PRAISE FOR THICH NHAT HANH

'He shows us the connection between personal, inner peace and peace on earth.'

— His Holiness the Dalai Lama

'Thich Nhat Hanh writes with the voice of the Buddha.'

— Sogyal Rinpoche

'Thich Nhat Hanh is more my brother than many who are nearer to me in race and nationality, because he and I see things the same exact way.'

— Thomas Merton

'Thich Nhat Hanh is a holy man, for he is humble and devout. He is (also) a scholar of immense intellectual capacity.'

— Martin Luther King

'Thich Nhat Hanh is a real poet.'

— Robert Lowell

'Thich Nhat Hanh is one of the most beloved Buddhist teachers in the West, a rare combination of mystic, poet, scholar and activist. His luminous presence and the simple, compassionate clarity of his writings have touched countless lives.'

— Joanna Macy

OTHER BOOKS BY THICH NHAT HANH

ANGER

Buddhist Wisdom for
Cooling the Flames

THICH NHAT HANH

RIDER

LONDON · SYDNEY · AUCKLAND · JOHANNESBURG

9 10 8

Copyright © 2001 by Thich Nhat Hanh

First published in 2001 by Riverhead Books, an imprint of Penguin Putnam Inc., USA
This edition published in 2001 by Rider, an imprint of Ebury Press, Random House, 20 Vauxhall Bridge Road, London SW1V 2SA
www.randomhouse.co.uk

Random House Australia (Pty) Limited
20 Alfred Street, Milsons Point, Sydney, New South Wales 2061, Australia

Random House New Zealand Limited
18 Poland Road, Glenfield, Auckland 10, New Zealand

Random House (Pty) Limited
Isle of Houghton, Corner of Boundary Road & Carse O'Gowrie
Houghton 2198, South Africa

Random House Publishers India Private Limited
301 World Trade Tower, Hotel Intercontinental Grand Complex, Barakhamba Lane, New Delhi 110 001, India

The Random House Group Limited Reg. No. 954009

Book design by Jennifer Ann Daddio

Papers used by Rider are natural, recyclable products made from wood grown in sustainable forests.

Printed and bound by Mackays of Chatham plc, Chatham, Kent

A CIP catalogue record for this book is available from the British Library

ISBN 9780712611817 (from January 2007)
ISBN 0712611819

CONTENTS

CONTENTS

INTRODUCTION

The Practice of Happiness

To be happy, to me, is to suffer less. If we were not capable of transforming the pain within ourselves, happiness would not be possible.

Many people look for happiness outside themselves, but true happiness must come from inside of us. Our culture tells us that happiness comes from having a lot of money, a lot of power, and a high position in society. But if you observe carefully, you will see that many rich and famous people are not happy. Many of them commit suicide.

The Buddha and the monks and nuns of his time did not own anything except their three robes and one bowl. But they were very happy, because they had something extremely precious—freedom.

According to the Buddha's teachings, the most basic condition for happiness is freedom. Here we do not mean political freedom, but freedom from the mental formations of anger, despair, jealousy, and delusion. These mental formations are described by the Buddha as poisons. As long as these poisons are still in our heart, happiness cannot be possible.

In order to be free from anger, we have to practice, whether we are Christian, Muslim, Buddhist, Hindu, or Jewish. We cannot ask the Buddha, Jesus, God, or Mohammed to take anger out of our hearts for us. There are concrete instructions on how to transform the craving, anger, and confusion within us. If we follow these instructions and learn to take good care of our suffering, we can help others do the same.

Making a Change for the Better

Suppose there is a family in which the father and son are angry with each other. They are not capable of communicating anymore. The father suffers a lot and also the son. They don't want to remain stuck in their anger, but they don't know how to overcome it.

A good teaching is the kind of teaching that you can apply directly to your life, so that you can transform your suffering. When you are angry, you suffer as though you are being burned by the fires of hell. When you feel great despair or jealousy, you are in hell. You have to go to a friend who practices, and ask how to practice in order to transform the anger, the despair in you.

Compassionate Listening Relieves Suffering

When a person's speech is full of anger, it is because he or she suffers deeply. Because he has so much suffering, he becomes full of bitterness. He is always ready to complain and blame others for his problems. This is why you find it very unpleasant to listen to him and try to avoid him.

To understand and transform anger, we must learn the practice of compassionate listening and using loving speech. There is a Bodhisattva—a Great Being or an Awakened person—who is capable of listening very deeply with a lot of compassion. She is called Kwan Yin or Avalokiteshvara, the

Bodhisattva of Great Compassion. We all must learn the practice of deep listening like this Bodhisattva. Then we can offer very concrete guidance to those who come seeking for help in order to restore communication.

Listening with compassion can help the other person to suffer less. Yet, even if you have the best intentions, you cannot listen deeply unless you train yourself in the art of compassionate listening. If you can sit down quietly and listen compassionately to that person for one hour, you can relieve a lot of his suffering. Listen with only one purpose: to allow the other person to express himself and find relief from his suffering. Keep compassion alive during the whole time of listening.

You have to be very concentrated while you listen. You have to focus on the practice of listening with all your attention, your whole being: your eyes, ears, body, and your mind. If you just pretend to listen, and do not listen with one hundred percent of yourself, the other person will know it and will not find relief from his suffering. If you know how to practice mindful breathing and can stay focused on the desire to help him find relief, then you will be able to sustain your compassion while listening.

Compassionate listening is a very deep practice. You listen not to judge or to blame. You listen just because you want the other person to suffer less. The other person might be our father, our son, our daughter, or our partner. Learning to listen to the other person can really help her to transform her anger and suffering.

A Bomb Ready to Explode

I know a Catholic woman who lives in North America. She suffered very much because she and her husband had a very difficult relationship. They were a well-educated family; they both had doctorate degrees. Yet the husband suffered so much. He was at war with his wife and all of his children. He could not talk to his wife or to his children. Everyone in the family tried to avoid him, because he was like a bomb ready to explode. His anger was enormous. He believed that his wife and his children despised him, because no one wanted to come near him. In fact, his wife did not despise him. His children did not despise him. They were afraid of him. To be close to him was dangerous because he could explode at any time.

One day the wife wanted to kill herself because she could not bear it any longer. She felt she was not able to continue living under these circumstances. But before she committed suicide, she called her friend who was a Buddhist practitioner to let her know what she was planning to do. The Buddhist friend had invited her several times to practice meditation in order to suffer less, but she had always refused. She explained that, as a Catholic, she could not practice or follow Buddhist teachings.

That afternoon, when the Buddhist woman learned that her friend was going to kill herself, she said over the telephone, "You claim to be my friend, and now you are about to die. The only thing I ask of you is to listen to the talk of my teacher, but you refuse. If you are really my friend, then please, take a taxi and come listen to the tape, and after that you can die."

When the Catholic woman arrived, her friend let her sit alone in the living room and listen to a dharma talk on restoring communication. During the hour or hour and a half that she listened to the dharma talk, she went through a very deep transformation within herself. She found out many things. She realized that she was partly responsible for her own suffering, and that she had also made her husband suffer a lot. She realized that she had not been able to help him at all. In fact, she had made his suffering heavier and heavier each day because she avoided him. She learned from the dharma talk that in order to help the other person, she should be able to listen deeply with compassion. That was something she had not been able to do in the last five years.

Defusing the Bomb

After listening to the dharma talk, the woman felt very inspired. She wanted to go home and practice deep listening in order to help her husband. But her Buddhist friend said, "No my friend, you should not do it today because compassionate listening is a very deep teaching. You have to train yourself for at least one or two weeks in order to be able to listen like a Bodhisattva." So the woman invited her Catholic friend to attend a retreat in order to learn more.

There were four hundred and fifty people participating in the retreat—eating, sleeping, and practicing together for six days. During that time, all of us practiced mindful breathing, aware of our in-breath and out-breath to bring our body and mind together. We practiced mindful walking, investing one hundred percent of ourselves in each step. We practiced mindful breathing, walking, and sitting in order to observe and embrace the suffering within us.

Not only did the participants listen to the dharma talks, but all of us practiced the art of listening to each other, and of using loving speech. We tried to listen deeply in order to understand the suffering of the other person. The Catholic woman practiced very seriously, very deeply, because for her, this was a matter of life or death.

When she returned home after the retreat, she was very calm, and her heart was full of compassion. She really wanted to help her husband to remove the bomb within his heart. She moved very slowly and followed her breathing to keep calm and nourish her compassion. She practiced walking mindfully, and her husband noticed that she was different. Finally, she came close and sat quietly next to him, something that she had never done in the last five years.

She was silent for a long time, maybe ten minutes. Then she gently put her hand on his and said, "My dear, I know you have suffered a lot during the last five years and I am very sorry. I know that I am greatly responsible for your suffering. Not only have I been unable to help you suffer less, but I have made the situation much worse. I have made many mistakes and caused you a great deal of pain. I am extremely sorry. I would like you to give me a chance to begin anew. I want to make you happy, but I have not known how to do it; that is why I have made the situation worse and worse every day. I don't want to continue like this anymore. So my darling, please help me. I need your help in order to understand you better, in order to love you better. Please tell me what is in your heart. I know you suffer a lot, I must know your suffering so that I will not do the wrong things again and again as in the past. Without you, I cannot do it. I need you to help me so that I will not continue to hurt you. I want only to love you." When she spoke to him like this, he began to cry. He cried like a little boy.

For a long time, his wife had been very sour. She always shouted and her speech had been full of anger, bitterness, blaming, and judging. They had only argued with each other. She had not spoken to him like this in years, with so much love and tenderness. When she saw her husband crying, she knew that now she had a chance. The door of her husband's heart had been closed, but now it was beginning to open again. She knew that she had to be very careful, so she continued her practice of mindful breathing. She said, "Please my dear, please tell me what is in your heart. I want to learn to do better so that I won't continue to make mistakes."

The wife is also an intellectual, she has a Ph.D. degree like her husband, but they suffered because neither of them knew how to practice listening to each other with compassion. But that night she was wonderful, she practiced compassionate listening successfully. It turned out to be a very healing night for both of them. After only a few hours together, they were able to reconcile with each other.

Right Teaching, Right Practice

If the practice is correct, if the practice is good, you don't need five or ten years, just a few hours may be enough to produce transformation and healing. I know that the Catholic woman was very successful that night, because she was able to convince her husband to sign up for a second retreat.

The second retreat lasted six days and at the end of the retreat, her husband also experienced a great transformation. During a tea meditation, he introduced his wife to the other retreatants. He said, "My dear friends, my dear co-practitioners, I would like to introduce to you a Bodhisattva, a Great Being. She is my wife, a great Bodhisattva. During the last five years, I have made her suffer so much, I have been so stupid. But, through her practice, she has changed everything. She has saved my life." After that they told their story and how they came to the retreat. They shared how they were able to reconcile on a deep level and renew their love.

When a farmer uses a kind of fertilizer that does not have any effect, he has to change the fertilizer. The same is true for us. If, after several months, the practice we are doing has not brought about any transformation and healing, we have to reconsider the situation. We must change our approach and learn more in order to find the right practice that can transform our life and the lives of the people we love.

All of us can do the same if we receive and learn the right teaching and the right practice. If you practice very seriously, if you make the practice a matter of life and death, like the Catholic woman, you can change everything.

Making Happiness Possible

We live in a time of many sophisticated means of communication. Information can travel to the other side of the planet very quickly. But it is exactly at this time that communication between people, father and son, husband and wife, mother and daughter, has become extremely difficult. If we cannot restore communication, happiness will never be possible. In the Buddhist teaching, the practice of compassionate listening, the practice of loving speech, and the practice of taking care of our anger are presented very clearly. We have to put into practice the teaching of the Buddha, concerning deep listening and loving speech in order to restore communication and bring happiness to our family, our school, and our community. Then we can help other people in the world.

ONE

❖

CONSUMING ANGER

We all need to know how to handle and take care of our anger. To do this, we must pay more attention to the bio-chemical aspect of anger, because anger has its roots in our body as well as our mind. When we analyze our anger, we can see its physiological elements. We have to look deeply at how we eat, how we drink, how we consume, and how we handle our body in our daily life.

Anger Is Not Strictly a Psychological Reality

In the teaching of the Buddha, we learn that our body and mind are not separate. Our body is our mind, and, at the same

13

time, our mind is also our body. Anger is not only a mental reality because the physical and the mental are linked to each other, and we cannot separate them. In Buddhism we call the body/mind formation *namarupa*. Namarupa is the psyche-soma, the mind-body as one entity. The same reality sometimes appears as mind, and sometimes appears as body.

Looking deeply into the nature of an elementary particle, scientists have discovered that sometimes it manifests as a wave, and sometimes as a particle. A wave is quite different from a particle. A wave can be only a wave. It cannot be a particle. A particle can be only a particle, it cannot be a wave. But the wave and the particle are the same thing. So instead of calling it a wave or a particle, they call it a "wavicle," combining the words *wave* and *particle*. This is the name scientists have given the elementary particle.

The same thing is true with mind and body. Our dualistic view tells us that mind cannot be body, and body cannot be mind. But looking deeply, we see that body is mind, mind is body. If we can overcome the duality that sees the mind and body as entirely separate, we come very close to the truth.

Many people are beginning to realize that what happens to the body also happens to the mind, and vice versa. Modern medicine is aware that the sickness of the body may be a result of sickness in the mind. And sickness in our minds may be connected to sickness in our bodies. Body and mind are not two separate entities—they are one. We have to take very good care of our body if we want to master our anger. The way we eat, the way we consume, is very important.

We Are What We Eat

Our anger, our frustration, our despair, have much to do with our body and the food we eat. We must work out a strategy of eating, of consuming to protect ourselves from anger and violence. Eating is an aspect of civilization. The way we grow our food, the kind of food we eat, and the way we eat it has much to do with civilization because the choices we make can bring about peace and relieve suffering.

The food that we eat can play a very important role in our anger. Our food may contain anger. When we eat the flesh of an animal with mad cow disease, anger is there in the meat. But we must also look at the other kinds of food that we eat. When we eat an egg or a chicken, we know that the egg or chicken can also contain a lot of anger. We are eating anger, and therefore we express anger.

Nowadays, chickens are raised in large-scale modern farms where they cannot walk, run, or seek food in the soil. They are fed solely by humans. They are kept in small cages and cannot move at all. Day and night they have to stand. Imagine that you have no right to walk or to run. Imagine that you have to stay day and night in just one place. You would become mad. So the chickens become mad.

In order for the chickens to produce more eggs, the farmers create artificial days and nights. They use indoor lighting to create a shorter day and a shorter night so that the chickens believe that twenty-four hours have passed, and then they produce more eggs. There is a lot of anger, a lot of frustration, and much suffering in the chickens. They express their anger and frustration by attacking the chickens next to them. They use their beaks to peck and wound each other. They cause each other to bleed, to suffer, and to die. That is why farmers now cut the beaks off all the chickens, to prevent them from attacking each other out of frustration.

So when you eat the flesh or egg of such a chicken, you are eating anger and frustration. So be aware. Be careful what you eat. If you eat anger, you will become and express anger. If you eat despair, you will express despair. If you eat frustration, you will express frustration.

We have to eat happy eggs from happy chickens. We have to drink milk that does not come from angry cows. We should drink organic milk that comes from cows that are raised naturally. We have to make an effort to support farmers to raise these animals in a more humane way. We also have to buy vegetables that are grown organically. It is more expensive, but, to compensate, we can eat less. We can learn to eat less.

Consuming Anger Through Other Senses

Not only do we nourish our anger with edible food, but also through what we consume with our eyes, ears, and consciousness. The consumption of cultural items is also linked to anger. Therefore, developing a strategy for consuming is very important.

What we read in magazines, what we view on television, can also be toxic. It may also contain anger and frustration. A film is like a piece of beefsteak. It can contain anger. If you consume it, you are eating anger, you are eating frustration. Newspaper articles, and even conversations, can contain a lot of anger.

You may feel lonely sometimes and want to talk to someone. In one hour of conversation, the other person's words may poison you with a lot of toxins. You may ingest a lot of anger, which you will express later on. That is why mindful consumption is very important. When you listen to the news, when you read a newspaper article, when you discuss something with others, are you ingesting the same kind of toxins that you ingest when you eat unmindfully?

Eating Well, Eating Less

There are those who take refuge in eating to forget their sorrow and their depression. Overeating can create difficulties for the digestive system, contributing to the arising of anger. It can also produce too much energy. If you do not know how to handle this energy, it can become the energy of anger, of sex, and of violence.

When we eat well, we can eat less. We need only half the amount of food that we eat every day. To eat well, we should chew our food about fifty times before we swallow. When we eat very slowly, and make the food in our mouth into a kind of liquid, we will absorb much more nutrition through our intestines. If we eat well, and chew our food carefully, we get more nutrition than if we eat a lot but don't digest it well.

Eating is a deep practice. When I eat, I enjoy every morsel of my food. I am aware of the food, aware that I am eating. We can practice mindfulness of eating—we know what we are chewing. We chew our food very carefully and with a lot of joy. From time to time, we stop chewing and get in touch with the friends, family, or sangha—community of practitioners—around us. We appreciate that it is wonderful to be sitting here chewing like this, not worrying about anything.

When we eat mindfully, we are not eating or chewing our anger, our anxiety, or our projects. We are chewing the food, prepared lovingly by others. It is very pleasant.

When the food in your mouth becomes almost liquefied, you experience its flavor more intensely and the food tastes very, very good. You may want to try chewing like this today. Be aware of each movement of your mouth. You will discover that the food tastes so delicious. It may only be bread. Without any butter or jelly at all. But it's wonderful. Perhaps you will also have some milk. I never drink milk. I chew milk. When I put a piece of bread into my mouth, I chew for a while in mindfulness, and then I take a spoonful of milk. I put it in my mouth, and I continue to chew with awareness. You don't know how delicious it can be just chewing some milk and some bread.

When the food has become liquid, mixed with your saliva, it is half digested already. So when it arrives in your stomach and intestines, the digestion becomes extremely easy. Much of the nutrients in the bread and milk will be absorbed into our body. You get a lot of joy and freedom during the time you chew. When you eat like this, you will naturally eat less.

When you serve yourself, be aware of your eyes. Don't trust them. It is your eyes that push you to take too much food. You don't need so much. If you know how to eat mindfully and joyfully, you become aware that you need only half the amount that your eyes tell you to take. Please try. Just chewing something very simple like zucchini, carrots, bread, and milk may turn out to be the best meal of your life. It's wonderful.

Many of us in Plum Village, our practice center in France, have experienced this kind of eating, chewing very mindfully, very slowly. Try eating like this. It can help you to feel much better in your body and, therefore, in your spirit, in your consciousness.

Our eyes are bigger than our stomach. We have to empower our eyes with the energy of mindfulness so that we know exactly what amount of food we really need. The Chinese term for the alms bowl used by a monk or nun means "the instrument for appropriate measure." We use this kind of bowl to protect us from being deceived by our eyes. If the food comes to the top of the bowl, we know that it is largely sufficient. We take only that amount of food. If you can eat like that, you can afford to buy less. When you buy less food, you can afford to buy organically grown food. This is something that we can do, alone or in our families. It will be a tremendous support for farmers who want to make a living growing organic food.

The Fifth Mindfulness Training

All of us need a diet based on our willingness to love and to serve. A diet based on our intelligence. The Five Mindfulness Trainings are the way out of suffering, for the world and for each of us as individuals (see full text in Appendix A). Looking deeply at the way we consume is the practice of the Fifth Mindfulness Training.

This mindfulness training concerns the practice of mindful consumption, of following a diet that can liberate us and liberate our society. Because we are aware of the suffering caused by unmindful consumption, we make the commitment:

> . . . to cultivate good health, both physical and mental, for myself, my family, and my society by practicing mindful eating, drinking, and consuming. I vow to ingest only items that preserve peace, well-being, and joy in my body, in my consciousness, and in the collective body and consciousness of my family and society. I am determined not to use alcohol or any other intoxicant or to ingest food or other items that contain toxins, such as certain TV programs, magazines, books, films, and conversations. . . ."

If you want to take care of your anger, your frustration, and your despair, you might consider living according to this mindfulness training. If you drink alcohol mindfully, you can see that it creates suffering. The intake of alcohol causes disease to the body and the mind, and deaths on the road. The making of alcohol also involves creating suffering. The use of the grains in its production is linked to the lack of food in the world. Mindfulness of eating and drinking can bring us this liberating insight.

Discuss a strategy of mindful consumption with the people you love, with members of your family, even if they are still young. Children can understand this, so they should participate in such discussions. Together you can make decisions about what to eat, what to drink, what television programs to watch, what to read, and what kind of conversations to have. This strategy is for your own protection.

We cannot speak about anger, and how to handle our anger, without paying attention to all the things that we consume, because anger is not separate from these things. Talk to your community about a strategy of mindful consuming. In Plum Village, we try our best to protect ourselves. We try not to consume things that nurture our anger, frustration, and fear. To consume more mindfully, we need to regularly discuss what we eat, how we eat, how to buy less, and how to have higher-quality food, both edible and the food we consume through our senses.

TWO

PUTTING OUT THE
FIRE OF ANGER

Saving Your House

When someone says or does something that makes us angry, we suffer. We tend to say or do something back to make the other suffer, with the hope that we will suffer less. We think, "I want to punish you, I want to make you suffer because you have made me suffer. And when I see you suffer a lot, I will feel better."

Many of us are inclined to believe in such a childish practice. The fact is that when you make the other suffer, he will try to find relief by making you suffer more. The result is an escalation of suffering on both sides. Both of you need compassion and help. Neither of you needs punishment.

When you get angry, go back to yourself, and take very good care of your anger. And when someone makes you suffer, go back and take care of your suffering, your anger. Do not say or do anything. Whatever you say or do in a state of anger may cause more damage in your relationship.

Most of us don't do that. We don't want to go back to ourselves. We want to follow the other person in order to punish him or her.

If your house is on fire, the most urgent thing to do is to go back and try to put out the fire, not to run after the person you believe to be the arsonist. If you run after the person you suspect has burned your house, your house will burn down while you are chasing him or her. That is not wise. You must go back and put out the fire. So when you are angry, if you continue to interact with or argue with the other person, if you try to punish her, you are acting exactly like someone who runs after the arsonist while everything goes up in flames.

Tools for Cooling the Flames

The Buddha gave us very effective instruments to put out the fire in us: the method of mindful breathing, the method of mindful walking, the method of embracing our anger, the method of looking deeply into the nature of our perceptions, and the method of looking deeply into the other person to realize that she also suffers a lot and needs help. These methods are very practical, and they come directly from Buddha.

To breathe in consciously is to know that the air is entering your body, and to breathe out consciously is to know that your body is exchanging air. Thus, you are in contact with the air and with your body, and because your mind is being attentive to all this, you are in contact with your mind, too; just as it is. It needs only one conscious breath to be back in contact with yourself and everything around you, and three conscious breaths to maintain the contact.

Whenever you are not standing, sitting, or lying down, you are going. But where are you going? You have already arrived. With every step, you can arrive in the present moment, you can step into the Pure Land or into the Kingdom of God. When you are walking from one side of the room to the other, or from one building to another, be aware of the contact of your feet with the earth and be aware of the contact of the air as it enters your body. It may help you to discover how many steps you can make comfortably during an in-breath and how many during an out-breath. As you breathe in, you can say "in," and as you breathe out, you can say "out." Then you are practicing walking meditation all day long. It is a practice, which is constantly possible and therefore has the power to transform our everyday life.

Many people like to read books about different spiritual traditions or to perform rituals but don't want to practice their teachings very much. The teachings can transform us no matter what religion or spiritual tradition we belong to, if we are only willing to practice. We will transform from a sea of fire into a refreshing lake. Then, not only do we stop suffering, but we also become a source of joy and happiness for many people around us.

What Do We Look Like When We're Angry?

Whenever anger comes up, take out a mirror and look at yourself. When you are angry, you are not very beautiful, you are not presentable. Hundreds of muscles on your face become very tense. Your face looks like a bomb ready to explode. Look at someone who is angry. When you see the tension in her, you become frightened. The bomb in her may explode any minute. So it is very helpful to see yourself in moments when you are angry. It is a bell of mindfulness. When you see yourself like that, you are motivated to do something to change it. You know what to do to look more beautiful. You don't need any cosmetics. You need only to breathe peacefully, calmly, and smile mindfully. If you can do that one or two times, you will look much better. Just look in the mirror, breathing in calmly, breathing out smiling, and you will feel relief.

Anger is a mental, psychological phenomenon, yet it is closely linked to biological and biochemical elements. Anger makes you tense your muscles, but when you know how to smile, you begin to relax and your anger will decrease. Smiling allows the energy of mindfulness to be born in you, helping you to embrace your anger.

In old times, servants of kings and queens always had to have a mirror, because whenever anyone was presented to the emperor, they had to be perfect in their appearance. So for the sake of formal etiquette, people would carry a pouch with a small mirror inside. Try it. Carry a mirror with you and look at it to see what state you are in. After you have breathed in and out a few times, smiling at yourself, the tension will be gone, and you will obtain some relief.

Embracing Anger with the Sunshine of Mindfulness

Anger is like a howling baby, suffering and crying. The baby needs his mother to embrace him. You are the mother for your baby, your anger. The moment you begin to practice breathing mindfully in and out, you have the energy of a mother, to cradle and embrace the baby. Just embracing your anger, just breathing in and breathing out, that is good enough. The baby will feel relief right away.

All plants are nourished by sunshine. All of them are sensitive to it. Any vegetation that is embraced by the sunshine will undergo a transformation. In the morning, the flowers have not yet opened. But when the sun comes out, the sunshine embraces the flowers and tries to penetrate them. The sunshine is made of tiny particles, photons. The photons gradually penetrate the flower one by one until there are a lot of them inside. At that point the flower cannot resist any longer and has to open herself to the sunshine.

In the same way, all mental formations and all physiological formations in us are sensitive to mindfulness. If mindfulness is there, embracing your body, your body will transform. If mindfulness is there, embracing your anger or despair, then they, too, will be transformed. According to the Buddha and according to our experience, anything embraced by the energy of mindfulness will undergo a transformation.

Your anger is like a flower. In the beginning you may not understand the nature of your anger, or why it has come up. But if you know how to embrace it with the energy of mindfulness, it will begin to open. You may be sitting, following your breathing, or you may be practicing walking meditation to generate the energy of mindfulness and embrace your anger. After ten or twenty minutes your anger will have to open herself to you, and suddenly, you will see the true nature of your anger. It may have arisen just because of a wrong perception or the lack of skillfulness.

Cooking Anger

You need to sustain your mindfulness for a certain amount of time in order for the flower of anger to open herself. It's like when you cook potatoes; you put the potatoes in the pot, cover it, and put it on the fire. But even with a very high flame, if you turn the fire off after five minutes, the potatoes will not be cooked. You have to keep the fire burning for at least fifteen or twenty minutes in order for the potatoes to cook. After that, you open the lid, and you smell the wonderful aroma of cooked potatoes.

Your anger is like that—it needs to be cooked. In the beginning it is raw. You cannot eat raw potatoes. Your anger is very difficult to enjoy, but if you know how to take care of it, to cook it, then the negative energy of your anger will become the positive energy of understanding and compassion.

You can do it. It is not something only a Great Being can

do. You can do it, too. You can transform the garbage of anger into the flower of compassion. Many of us can do this in just fifteen minutes. The secret is to continue the practice of mindful breathing, the practice of mindful walking, generating the energy of mindfulness in order to embrace your anger.

Embrace your anger with a lot of tenderness. Your anger is not your enemy, your anger is your baby. It's like your stomach or your lungs. Every time you have some trouble in your lungs or your stomach, you don't think of throwing them away. The same is true with your anger. You accept your anger because you know you can take care of it; you can transform it into positive energy.

Turning Garbage Into Flowers

The organic gardener does not think of throwing away the garbage. She knows that she needs the garbage. She is capable of transforming the garbage into compost, so that the compost can turn into lettuce, cucumbers, radishes, and flowers again. As a practitioner, you are a kind of gardener, an organic gardener.

Anger and love are both of an organic nature, and that means they both can change. Love can be transformed into hate. You know this very well. Many of us begin a relationship with great love, very intense love. So intense that we believe that, without our partner, we cannot survive. Yet if we do not practice mindfulness, it takes only one or two years for our love to be transformed into hatred. Then, in our partner's presence we have the opposite feeling, we feel terrible. It becomes impossible to live together anymore, so divorce is the only way. Love has been transformed into hatred; our flower has become garbage. But with the energy of mindfulness, you can look into the garbage and say, "I am not afraid. I am capable of transforming the garbage back into love."

If you see elements of garbage in you, like fear, despair, and hatred, don't panic. As a good organic gardener, a good practitioner, you can face this: "I recognize that there is garbage in me. I am going to transform this garbage into nourishing compost that can make love reappear."

Those who have confidence in the practice don't think of running away from a difficult relationship. When you know the techniques of mindful breathing, mindful walking, mindful sitting, and mindful eating, you can generate the energy of mindfulness and embrace your anger or your despair. Just embracing it will give you relief. Then as you continue embracing, you can practice looking deeply into the nature of your anger.

So the practice has two phases. The first phase is embracing and recognizing: "My dear anger, I know you are there, I am taking good care of you." The second phase is to look deeply into the nature of your anger to see how it has come about.

Caring for Your Baby, Anger

You have to be like a mother listening for the cries of her baby. If a mother is working in the kitchen and hears her baby crying, she puts down whatever she is doing, and goes to comfort her baby. She may be making a very good soup; the soup is important, but it's much less important than the suffering of her baby. She has to put down the soup, and go the baby's room. Her appearance in the room is like sunshine because the mother is full of warmth, concern, and tenderness. The first thing she does is pick up the baby and embrace him tenderly. When the mother embraces her baby, her energy penetrates him and soothes him. This is exactly what you have to learn to do when anger begins to surface. You have to abandon everything that you are doing, because your most important task is to go back to yourself and take care of your baby, your anger. Nothing is more urgent than taking good care of your baby.

Remember when you were a little child and you had a fever, although they gave you aspirin or other medicine, you didn't feel better until your mother came and put her hand on your burning forehead? That felt so good! Her hand was like the hand of a goddess. When she touched you with her hand, a lot of freshness, love, and compassion penetrated into your body. The hand of your mother is your own hand. Her hand is still alive in yours, if you know how to breathe in and out, to be mindful. Then, touching your forehead with your very own hand, you will see that your mother's hand is still there, touching your forehead. You will have the same energy of love and tenderness for yourself.

The mother holds her baby with mindfulness, fully concentrated on him. The baby feels some relief because he is being held tenderly by his mother, like the flower embraced by the sunshine. She holds the baby not only for the sake of holding the baby, but also to find out what is wrong with him. Because she is a true mother, and very talented, she can find out what is wrong with her baby very quickly. She is a baby specialist.

As practitioners, we have to be anger specialists. We have to attend to our anger; we have to practice until we understand the roots of our anger and how it works.

Holding Your Baby

Holding the baby mindfully, the mother quickly discovers the cause of his suffering. Then it is very easy for her to correct the situation. If the baby has a fever, then she will give him medicine to help the fever go down. If he is hungry, she will feed him warm milk. If the diaper is too tight, she will loosen it.

As practitioners, we do exactly like this. We hold our baby of anger in mindfulness so that we get relief. We continue the practice of mindful breathing and mindful walking, as a lullaby for our anger. The energy of mindfulness penetrates into the energy of anger, exactly like the energy of the mother penetrates into the energy of the baby. There's no difference at all. If you know how to practice mindful breathing, smiling, and walking meditation, it is certain that you will find relief in five, ten, or fifteen minutes.

Discovering the True Nature of Your Anger

At the moment you become angry, you tend to believe that your misery has been created by another person. You blame him or her for all your suffering. But by looking deeply, you may realize that the seed of anger in you is the main cause of your suffering. Many other people, confronted with the same situation, would not get angry like you. They hear the same words, they see the same situation, and yet they are able to stay calm and not be carried away. Why do you get angry so easily? You may get angry very easily because your seed of anger is too strong. And because you have not practiced the methods for taking good care of your anger, the seed of anger has been watered too often in the past.

All of us have a seed of anger in the depth of our consciousness. But in some of us, that seed of anger is bigger than our other seeds—like love or compassion. The seed of anger may be bigger because we have not practiced in the past. When we begin to cultivate the energy of mindfulness, the first insight we have is that the main cause of our suffering, of our misery, is not the other person—it is the seed of anger in us. Then we will stop blaming the other person for causing all our suffering. We realize she or he is only a secondary cause.

You get a lot of relief when you have this kind of insight, and you begin to feel much better. But the other person still may be in hell because she does not know how to practice. Once you have taken care of your anger, you become aware that she is still suffering. So now you can focus your attention on the other person.

Helping Not Punishing

When someone does not know how to handle his own suffering, he allows it to spill all over the people around him. When you suffer, you make people around you suffer. That's very natural. This is why we have to learn how to handle our suffering, so we won't spread it everywhere.

When you are the head of a family, for instance, you know that the well-being of your family members is very important. Because you have compassion, you do not allow your suffering to harm those around you. You practice to learn how to handle your suffering because you know that your suffering is not an individual matter, your happiness is not an individual matter.

When someone is angry, and doesn't know how to handle her anger, she is helpless, she suffers. She also makes the people around her suffer. At first, you feel that she deserves punishment. You want to punish her because she has made you suffer. But after ten or fifteen minutes of walking meditation and mindful looking, you realize that what she needs is help and not punishment. This is a good insight.

This person may be someone very close to you—she may be your wife, he may be your husband. If you don't help him or her, who will?

Because you know how to embrace your anger, you now feel much better, but you see that the other person continues to suffer. This insight motivates you to go back to him. No one can help, except you. Now you are filled with the desire to return and help. It is a completely different kind of thinking—there is no more wish to punish. Your anger has been transformed into compassion.

The practice of mindfulness leads to concentration and insight. Insight is the fruit of the practice, which can help us to forgive, to love. In a period of fifteen minutes, or half an hour, the practice of mindfulness, concentration, and insight can liberate you from your anger and turn you into a loving person. That is the strength of the dharma, the miracle of the dharma.

Stopping the Cycle of Anger

There was a twelve-year-old boy who used to come to Plum Village every summer to practice with other young people. He had a problem with his father because every time he made a mistake or fell and hurt himself, instead of helping, his father would shout at him and call him all sorts of names: "You stupid boy! How can you do something like that to yourself?" This would happen just because the boy would fall down and get hurt. So he didn't see his father as a loving father, as a good father. He promised himself that when he grew up, got married, and had children, he would not treat his children like that. If his son was playing and got hurt and bled, he would not shout at him. He would embrace his son and try to help him.

The second year he was in Plum Village, he came with his younger sister. His sister was playing with other girls on the hammock, and suddenly she fell off. She hit her head on a piece of rock, and blood began to stream down her face. Suddenly the young man felt the energy of anger coming up. He was about to shout at his younger sister: "You stupid girl! How could you do something like that to yourself?" He was about to do the same thing that his father had done to him. But because he had practiced in Plum Village for two summers, he was able to stop himself. Instead of shouting, he began to practice mindful walking and mindful breathing while others helped his sister. In just five minutes he experienced a moment of enlightenment. He saw that his reaction, his anger, was a kind of habit energy that had been transmitted to him by his father. He had become exactly like his father, the continuation of his father. He did not want to treat his sister like that, but the energy transmitted to him by his father was so strong that he almost did exactly what his father had done to him.

For a twelve-year-old boy, that is quite an awakening. He continued his walking, and suddenly he was filled with the desire to practice in order to transform this habit energy, so that he would not transmit it to his children. He knew that only the practice of mindfulness could help him to stop this cycle of suffering.

The boy was also able to see that his father was a victim of the transmission of anger as well. His father might not have wanted to treat him like that, but he had done so because the habit energy in him was too strong. The moment this insight came to him, that his father was also a victim of transmission, all of his anger toward his father vanished. A few minutes later, he suddenly had the desire to go back home and invite his father to practice with him. As a young man of twelve years old, that was quite a realization.

A Good Gardener

When you understand the suffering of the other person, you are able to transform your desire to punish, and then you want only to help him or her. At that moment, you know that your practice has succeeded. You are a good gardener.

Inside every one of us is a garden, and each practitioner has to go back to it and take care of it. Maybe in the past, you left it untended for a long time. You should know exactly what is going on in your own garden, and try to put everything in order. Restore the beauty; restore the harmony in your garden. Many people will enjoy your garden, if it is well tended.

Taking Care of Yourself, Taking Care of the Other

As children, our fathers and our mothers taught us how to breathe, how to walk, how to sit, how to eat, and how to speak. But when we come to the practice, we are reborn, as spiritual beings. So we have to learn how to breathe again, mindfully. We learn how to walk again, mindfully. We want to learn how to listen again, mindfully and with compassion. We want to learn how to speak again, with the language of love, to honor our original commitment. "Darling, I suffer. I am angry. I want you to know it." This expresses faithfulness to your commitment. "Darling, I am doing my best. I am taking good care of my anger. For me and for you also. I don't want to explode, to destroy myself and destroy you. I am doing my best. I am putting into practice what I have learned from my teacher, from my sangha." This faithfulness will inspire respect and confidence in the other party. And lastly,

"Darling, I need your help." This is a very strong statement, because usually when you're angry, you have the tendency to say, "I don't need you."

If you can say these three sentences with sincerity, from your heart, a transformation will take place in the other person. You cannot doubt the effect of such a practice. You influence the other person to start practicing, too, just by your behavior. She will think, "He is faithful to me. He is keeping his commitment. He is trying to do his best. I must do the same."

So in taking good care of yourself, you take good care of your beloved one. Self-love is the foundation for your capacity to love the other person. If you don't take good care of yourself, if you are not happy, if you are not peaceful, you cannot make the other person happy. You cannot help the other person; you cannot love. Your capacity for loving another person depends entirely on your capacity for loving yourself, for taking care of yourself.

Healing the Wounded Child Within

Many of us still have a wounded child alive within us. Our wounds may have been caused by our father or our mother. Our father may have been wounded when he was a child. Our mother may have been wounded as a little girl, too. Because they did not know how to heal the wounds from their childhood, they have transmitted their wounds to us. If we do not know how to transform and heal the wounds in ourselves, we are going to transmit them to our children and grandchildren. This is why we have to go back to the wounded child in us, to help him or her heal.

Sometimes the wounded child in us needs all of our attention. That little child might emerge from the depths of our consciousness, and ask for our attention. If you are mindful, you will hear his or her voice calling for help. At that moment, instead of contemplating the beautiful sunrise, you go back and tenderly embrace the wounded child within you. "Breathing in, I go back to my wounded child; breathing out, I will take good care of my wounded child."

To take good care of ourselves, we must go back and take care of the wounded child inside of us. You have to practice going back to your wounded child every day. You have to embrace him or her tenderly, like a big brother or a big sister. You have to talk to him, talk to her. And you can write a letter to the little child in you, of two or three pages, to say that you recognize his or her presence and you will do everything you can to heal his or her wounds.

When we speak of listening with compassion, we usually think of listening to someone else. But we must also listen to the wounded child inside of us. The wounded child in us is here in the present moment. And we can heal him or her right now. "My dear little wounded child, I'm here for you, ready to listen to you. Please tell me all your suffering, all your pain. I am here, really listening." And if you know how to go back to her, to him, and listen like that every day for five or ten minutes, healing will take place. When you climb a beautiful mountain, invite your little child within to climb with you. When you contemplate the beautiful sunset, invite him or her to enjoy it with you. If you do that for a few weeks or a few months, the wounded child in you will be healed. Mindfulness is the energy that can help us do this.

Becoming a Free Person

One minute of practice is one minute of generating the energy of mindfulness. It doesn't come from outside of you; it comes from within. The energy of mindfulness is the kind of energy that helps us to be here, to be fully present in the here and the now. When you drink tea in mindfulness, your body and your mind are perfectly united. You are real, and the tea you drink also becomes real. When you sit in a café, with a lot of music in the background and a lot of projects in your head, you're not really drinking your coffee or your tea. You're drinking your projects, you're drinking your worries. You are not real, and the coffee is not real either. Your tea or your coffee can only reveal itself to you as a reality when you go back to your self, and produce your true presence, freeing yourself from the past, the future, and from your worries. When you are real, the tea also becomes real and the encounter between you and the tea is real. This is genuine tea drinking.

You can organize a tea meditation to provide an opportunity for your friends to practice being truly present in order to enjoy a cup of tea and each other's presence. Tea meditation is a practice. It is a practice to help us be free. If you are still bound and haunted by the past, if you are still afraid of the future, if you are carried away by your projects, your fear, your anxiety, and your anger, you are not a free person. You are not fully present in the here and the now, so life is not really available to you. The tea, the other person, the blue sky, the flower, is not available to you. In order to be really alive, in order to touch life deeply, you have to become a free person. Cultivating mindfulness can help you to be free.

The energy of mindfulness is the energy of being present. Body and mind united. When you practice mindful breathing or mindful walking, you become free of the past, free of the future, free of your projects, and you become totally alive and present again. Freedom is the basic condition for you to touch life, to touch the blue sky, the trees, the birds, the tea, and the other person. This is why mindfulness practice is very important. Yet it is not something that you have to train yourself for many months to be able to do. One hour of practice can help you to be more mindful. Train yourself to drink your tea mindfully, to become a free person while drinking tea. Train yourself to be a free person while you make breakfast. Any moment of the day is an opportunity for you to train yourself in mindfulness and to generate this energy.

"Darling, I Know You Are There, and I Am Very Happy"

With mindfulness, you can recognize what is there in the present moment, including the person you love. When you can tell your beloved, "Darling, I know you are there, and I am very happy," it proves that you are a free person. It proves that you have mindfulness, you have the capacity to cherish, to appreciate what is happening in the present moment. What is happening in the present moment is life. You are still alive and the person you love is still there, alive, in front of you.

The amount of mindfulness you cultivate in yourself is very important. You embrace the other person with this energy of mindfulness. You look at her or him lovingly and you say, "Darling, it is wonderful that you are here, alive. It makes me very happy." Not only are you happy, but the other person is happy, too, because she or he has been embraced by your mindfulness. When you can be with the other person in this way, the chances of getting angry are already much smaller.

Anyone can practice this; and you do not have to practice eight months in order to do it. You need only one or two minutes of mindful breathing or mindful walking, in order to reestablish yourself in the here and the now, to be alive again. Then you go to the other person, you look into his eyes, you smile, and you make this declaration, "Darling, it is so wonderful that you are here, alive. It makes me very happy."

Mindfulness makes you and the other person happy and free. The other person may be caught in her worries, anger, and forgetfulness, but with mindfulness you can save her and yourself. Mindfulness is the energy of the Buddha, the energy of enlightenment. The Buddha is present whenever you are mindful, embracing both of you in his loving arms.

THREE

THE LANGUAGE OF TRUE LOVE

A Peace Talk

We practice with our family, we practice with our spiritual friends because alone we cannot succeed easily. We need allies. In the past, we were allied in making each other suffer more, allied in the escalation of anger. Now we want to be allied in taking good care of our sorrow, our anger, and our frustration. We want to negotiate a strategy for peace.

Start a peace talk with your beloved one: "Darling, in the past we have made each other suffer so much. Both of us were victims of our anger. We made a hell for each other. Now, I want to change. I want us to become allies, so that we can protect each other, practice together, and transform our anger together. Let us build a better life from now on, based on the practice of mindfulness. Darling, I need your help. I need your support. I need your collaboration. I cannot succeed without you." You have to say these words to your partner, your son, your daughter—it's time to do it. This is awakening. This is love.

You may attain some enlightenment just by listening to five minutes of a dharma talk. But you have to maintain that enlightenment in your daily life, so that you can bring it home and begin to apply it to your daily life. As enlightenment grows in you, confusion and ignorance will have to withdraw. It will not only influence your thinking, but also your body and your way of living. So it is very important to go to your partner, to your beloved one, and negotiate a strategy of peace, a strategy of consuming, a strategy of protection. You have to bring the best of yourself: your talent, your skillfulness, everything, in order to succeed at this negotiation table so that you will no longer make each other suffer. You want to begin anew, you want to transform yourself. It's up to you to convince the other person.

Reestablishing Communication

There is a young American who did not speak with his father for five years. Conversation was entirely impossible. One day he came in contact with the dharma, and it had a deep impact on him. He wanted to begin anew, to change his life. So he decided to become a monk. With great eagerness to learn, he stayed with the Plum Village sangha for three or four months, and he proved he was capable of becoming a monk. From the day he came to our center, he practiced mindful consumption, walking meditation, sitting meditation, participating in all the activities of the sangha.

He did not expect anything from his father, he just began with himself. Thanks to that kind of living, making peace with himself, he was able to write his father every week. Not expecting an answer at all, he wrote to his father about his practice, the small joys he felt every day. Six months later, he picked up the phone, and breathed in and out mindfully. This helped him to stay calm. He dialed the number, and his father answered. His father knew that he had become a monk, and he was very angry about that. So the first thing he said was, "Are you still with that group? Are you still a monk? What is your future?" The young man replied, "Dad, my greatest concern now is how to establish a good relationship between us. That would make me very happy. It is the most important thing to me. To be able to communicate with you again, to be able to be close again, that is my only concern. It is more important than anything, including the future."

His father kept silent, for a long time. The young monk

just continued to follow his breathing. Finally the father said, "Okay, I accept that. That is important for me, too." So anger was not the only thing his father felt for his son. In many letters, the young man had written about beautiful things that had nourished the positive elements in his father. From that day on, his father called him every week. Communication has been reestablished, and the happiness of both father and son has now become a reality.

Peace Begins with You

Before we can make deep changes in our lives, we have to look into our diet, our way of consuming. We have to live in such a way that we stop consuming the things that poison us and intoxicate us. Then, we will have the strength to allow the best in us to arise, and we will no longer be victims of anger, of frustration.

Everything is possible when the door of communication is open. So we must invest ourselves in the practice of opening up and restoring communication. You have to express your willingness, your desire to make peace with the other person. Ask him to support you. Tell him, "Communication between us is the most important thing to me. Our relation-

ship is the most precious thing, nothing is more important."
Make it clear and ask for support.

You have to start negotiating a strategy. No matter how much the other person can do, you have to do all that you are capable of doing yourself. You must give one hundred percent of yourself. Whatever you can do for yourself, you do for him, or for her. Don't wait. Don't put forth conditions, saying, "If you don't make an effort to reconcile, then I won't either." This will not work. Peace, reconciliation, and happiness begin with you.

It is wrong to think that if the other person does not change or improve, then nothing can be improved. There are always ways to create more joy, peace, and harmony, and you have access to them. The way you walk, the way you breathe, the way you smile, the way you react, all of this is very important. You must begin with this.

There are many ways to communicate, and the best way is to show that you no longer feel any anger or condemnation. You show that you understand and accept the other person. You communicate this not only by your words, but also by your way of being—with your eyes full of compassion and your actions full of tenderness. The fact that you are fresh and pleasant to be around already changes a lot. No one can resist coming close to you. You become a tree with a cool shade, a stream of cool water. Both people and animals will want to come near you because your presence is refreshing and enjoyable. When you begin with yourself, you will be able to restore communication, and the other person will change naturally.

Peace Treaty

We tell our beloved one, "My darling, in the past we have made each other suffer so much, because neither of us was capable of handling our anger. Now we have to work out a strategy for taking good care of our anger."

The dharma can remove the heat of anger, and the fever of suffering. It is a wisdom that can bring joy and peace in the here and the now. Our strategy for peace and reconciliation should be based on this.

Whenever the energy of anger comes up, we often want to express it to punish the person whom we believe to be the source of our suffering. This is the habit energy in us. When we suffer, we always blame the other person for having made us suffer. We do not realize that anger is, first of all, our business. We are primarily responsible for our anger, but we believe very naively that if we can say something or do something to punish the other person, we will suffer less. This kind of belief should be uprooted. Because whatever you do or say in a state of anger will only cause more damage in the relationship. Instead, we should try not to do anything or say anything when we are angry.

When you say something really unkind, when you do something in retaliation, your anger increases. You make the other person suffer, and he will try hard to say or do something back to get relief from his suffering. That is how the conflict escalates. This has happened so many times in the past. You are both very familiar with the escalation of anger, of suffering, and yet you have not learned anything from it. Trying to punish the other person is only going to make the situation worse.

Punishing the other person is self-punishment. That is true in every circumstance. Every time the United States Army tries to punish Iraq, not only does Iraq suffer, but the U.S. also suffers. Every time Iraq tries to punish the U.S., the U.S. suffers, but Iraq also suffers. The same is true everywhere; between the Israeli and Palestinian, between the Muslim and Hindu, between you and the other person. It has always been like that. So let us wake up; let us be aware that punishing the other is not an intelligent strategy. Both you and the other person are intelligent. You can use your intelligence. You must come together and agree on a strategy for taking care of your anger. You both know that trying to punish each other is not wise. So promise each other that every time you get angry, you will not say or do anything out of anger. Instead, you will take care of your anger by going back to yourselves—practicing mindful breathing and mindful walking.

Take advantage of the moments when you are happy together to sign the contract, your peace treaty, a treaty of true love. Your peace treaty should be written and signed entirely on the basis of love, not like a peace treaty signed by political parties. They base their treaties only on national self-interest. They are still full of a lot of suspicion and anger. But your peace treaty must be purely a love treaty.

Embracing Anger

The Buddha never advised us to suppress our anger. He taught us to go back to ourselves and take good care of it. When something is physically wrong with us, in our intestines, our stomach, or our liver, we have to stop and take good care of them. We do some massage, we use a hot-water bottle, we do everything possible in order to take care of them.

Just like our organs, our anger is part of us. When we are angry, we have to go back to ourselves and take good care of our anger. We cannot say, "Go away anger, you have to go away. I don't want you." When you have a stomachache, you don't say, "I don't want you stomach, go away." No, you take care of it. In the same way, we have to embrace and take good care of our anger. We recognize it as it is, embrace it, and smile. The energy that helps us do these things is mindfulness, mindfulness of walking and mindfulness of breathing.

Happiness Is Not an Individual Matter

This does not mean that you have to hide your anger. You have to let the other person know that you are angry and that you suffer. This is very important. When you get angry with someone, please don't pretend that you are not angry. Don't pretend that you don't suffer. If the other person is dear to you, then you have to confess that you are angry, and that you suffer. Tell him or her in a calm way.

In true love, there is no pride. You cannot pretend that you don't suffer. You cannot pretend that you are not angry. This kind of denial is based on pride. "Angry? Me? Why should I be angry? I'm okay." But, in fact, you are not okay. You are in hell. Anger is burning you up, and you must tell your partner, your son, your daughter. Our tendency is to say, "I don't need you to be happy! I can be on my own!" This is a betrayal of our initial vow to share everything.

In the beginning you told each other, "I cannot live without you. My happiness depends on you." You made declarations like that. But when you are angry, you say the opposite: "I don't need you! Don't come near me! Don't touch me!" You prefer to go into your room and lock the door. You try your best to demonstrate that you don't need the other person. This is a very human, very ordinary tendency. But this is not wisdom. Happiness is not an individual matter. If one of you is not happy, it will be impossible for the other person to be happy.

I. "DARLING, I AM ANGRY. I SUFFER."

To say, "Darling, I love you," is good, it is important. It is natural that we share our joy and good feelings with our beloved one. But you also have to let the other person know when you suffer, when you are angry with him or her. You have to express what you feel. You have the right. This is true love. "Darling, I am angry at you. I suffer." Try your best to say it peacefully. There may be some sadness in your voice, that's fine. Just don't say something to punish or to blame. "Darling, I am angry. I suffer, and I need you to know it." This is the language of love, because you have vowed to support each other, as partners, or as husband and wife. Father and son, mother and daughter are also a couple, so even if the other person is your child or your parent, you must still speak out.

You have the duty to tell him or her when you suffer. When you are happy, share your happiness, with her, with him. When you suffer, tell your beloved one about your suffering. Even if you think your anger was created by him or her, you still have to keep your commitment. Tell him or her calmly. Use loving speech. This is the only condition.

You must do this as soon as possible. You should not keep your anger, your suffering to yourself for more than twenty-four hours. Otherwise, it becomes too much. It can poison you. This would prove that your love, your trust for him or her is very weak. So you have to tell him or her about your suffering, your anger as soon as you can. Twenty-four hours is the deadline.

You may feel you are not capable of telling him or her right away because you are not yet calm. You are still very angry. So practice mindful breathing and walking outdoors. Then when you feel calm and ready to share, you speak. But if the deadline comes close, and you are not yet calm, then you have to write it down. Write a Peace Note, a peace message. Deliver the letter to her and make sure she gets it before twenty-four hours have passed. This is very important. Each of you has to make the promise to act in this way when you get angry at each other. Otherwise you are not respecting the terms of your peace treaty.

2. "I AM DOING MY BEST."

If you are committed to changing things, you can go further. You can add another sentence when you let the other person know that you suffer. You can add, "I'm doing my best." This means you refrain from acting out of anger. It means that you are practicing mindful breathing and mindful walking in order to embrace your anger with mindfulness. You are practicing according to the teaching. Don't say, "I am doing my best" unless you practice. When you are angry, you know how to practice, so you have the right to say, "I am doing my best." That will inspire confidence and respect in the other person. "I am doing my best" means you are living up to your commitment to go home to yourself and take good care of your anger.

When you are angry, your anger is your baby and you have to look after it. It is like when your stomach is upset, you have to go back to yourself and embrace your stomach. Your stomach is your baby at that moment. Our stomach is a physical formation, a physiological formation, and our anger is a mental formation. We must take care of our anger in the same way we take care of our stomach or kidneys. You cannot say, "Anger, go away, you don't belong to me." So when you say, "I am doing my best," it is because you are embracing and taking good care of your anger. You are practicing mindful breathing and walking to release the energy of anger and transform it into positive energy.

While embracing your anger, you practice looking deeply to see the nature of your anger because you know that you may be the victim of a wrong perception. You may have misunderstood what you heard and what you saw. You may have a wrong idea of what had been said, what had been done. Your anger is born from such ignorance and wrong perceptions. When you say "I am doing my best," you are aware that in the past you have gotten angry many times because of your wrong perception of what was going on. So now you are very careful. You remember that you should not be so sure that you are the victim of the other person's wrongdoing, the victim of the other person's words. You yourself may have created the hell inside you.

3. "PLEASE HELP ME."

The third sentence follows naturally, "Please help me. Darling, I need your help." That is the language of true love. When you get angry with the other person, you have the tendency to say the opposite—"Don't touch me! I don't need you. I can manage very well without you!" But you have made the commitment to take good care of each other. So it's very natural that when you suffer, although you know how to practice, you still need the other person to help you in your practice. "Darling, I need your help. Please do help me."

If you are capable of writing or saying these three sentences, you are capable of true love. You are using the authentic language of love. "Darling, I suffer, and I want you to know it. Darling, I am doing my best. I'm trying not to blame anyone else, including you. Since we are so close to each other, since we have made a commitment to each other, I feel that I need your support and your help to get out of this state of suffering, of anger." Using the three sentences to communicate with the other person can quickly reassure and relieve him or her. The way you handle your anger will inspire a lot of confidence and respect in the other person, and in yourself. This is not very difficult to do.

Transforming Anger Together

If I were the other person, and you shared these three sentences with me, I would see that you are very faithful to me, that you really have true love for me. Not only when you're happy do you share your happiness, but when you suffer, you also share your suffering. When you tell me you are doing your best, I have confidence and I respect you because you are a real practitioner. You are faithful to what you have learned, the teachings and your community of practice. When you practice these three sentences, you are embracing your teacher and your sangha in your heart.

Because you are doing your best, I end up doing my best. I go back to myself and practice. In order to be worthy of you, I have to look deeply, and also do my best. I have to ask myself, "What did I say, what did I do to have made her or him suffer like that? Why did I do that?" Just listening to you, just reading the Peace Note you gave me, I can recover myself. The dharma, after having touched you, is now beginning to touch me, and it is my turn to be inhabited by the energy of mindfulness.

So when the other person receives your message, a message communicated by loving speech, he will be inspired by your love, by your language, and by your practice. A lot of awakening and respect is born in him when the message has gotten across. He will be willing to go back to himself and reconsider whether he has done or said anything that has made you suffer. In this way you have conveyed to him your practice. He will see that you are doing your best. And in order to respond to that, he also will want to do his best. He will say silently to himself: "Darling, I am also doing my best."

This is wonderful; both of you are practicing. The dharma has inhabited both of you. The Buddha is alive in each of you. There is no danger anymore. You have come back to yourself, practicing looking deeply in order to truly understand the situation. If during this time, one of you experiences an insight into what is really going on, then you have to tell the other person right away what you have discovered.

Perhaps you become aware that you became angry because of a wrong perception. When you have such an insight, you have to tell the other person right away. You must let her know that you are sorry that you got angry for nothing. She did not do anything wrong at all. You got angry because you misunderstood the situation. Telephone her, fax her, e-mail her, because she is still very concerned about your suffering. This will give her relief right away.

In looking back, the other person may also realize that she has said or done something out of irritation or because of a wrong perception. She regrets what she has said or done to you, and so she also has to share her insight. "Darling, the other day, I was not very mindful. I said something incorrect. I had a misperception. I did something unkind, and I see it was because I was not skillful enough. I did not mean to make you suffer. So I apologize and I promise that next time, I'll be more skillful, more mindful." When you get this message, you stop suffering, and in your heart, you feel a lot of respect for the other person. Now, the other person is a co-practitioner. Your mutual respect for each other continues to grow, and respect is the foundation of true love.

The Special Guest

In the Vietnamese tradition, husband and wife are expected to treat each other like a guest. You really respect each other. When you change your clothes, you don't change in front of each other. You behave with reverence. If respect for the other person is no longer there, true love cannot continue for long. Respecting each other, treating each other as a guest, is traditional in Asian society. I believe this attitude existed in the West also, at least in old times. Without such mutual respect, love cannot last for a long time. Anger and other negative energies will begin to dominate.

In the wedding ceremonies performed in Plum Village, our retreat center in France, the couple bows to each other, to show their respect. This is because each person has the Buddha nature within—the capacity to be enlightened, to develop great compassion and great understanding. When you bow to your partner with respect, you notice your love. If you no longer have any respect for the other person, love is dead. This is why we have to be very careful to nourish and sustain our mutual respect.

Using these three sentences of true love, looking deeply to acknowledge our responsibility in the conflict, is a very concrete way to express our respect and nourish our love. Do not underestimate the three sentences of true love.

Pebble in Your Pocket

Every molecule of these three sentences consists entirely of true love. Love can handle anything. You may like to write these three sentences down on a piece of paper the size of a credit card and slip it into your wallet. Revere that sheet of paper as something that can save you because it will remind you of your commitment to each other.

Some of us keep a pebble in our pocket, a beautiful pebble we picked up in the front yard. We washed it very carefully and always carry it with us. Every time we put our hands in our pocket, we touch the small pebble, and hold it gently. We practice mindful breathing and we feel very peaceful. When anger arises, the pebble becomes the dharma. It reminds us of our three sentences. Just holding the pebble, breathing in and out calmly and smiling, can help you tremendously. It sounds a little bit childish, but this practice is very useful. When you are in school, at work, or out shopping, you have no reminders to bring you back to yourself. So the little pebble in your pocket serves as your teacher, as your fellow practitioner—it is a bell of mindfulness, allowing you to pause and return to your breathing.

Many people invoke the name of Jesus or Buddha Amitabha with a rosary. The pebble is a kind of rosary, a reminder that your teacher is always with you, your dharma brothers and sisters are always with you. It will help you to go back to your breathing, allow love to be born in you, and keep that love in you alive. It can help keep enlightenment alive in you.

FOUR

TRANSFORMATION

Zones of Energy

We know that when anger is present in us we should refrain from reacting, namely from speaking, or doing anything. To say something, to do something while you are angry is not wise. We are urged to go back to ourselves in order to take good care of our anger.

Anger is a zone of energy in us. It is part of us. It is a suffering baby that we have to take care of. The best way to do this is to generate another zone of energy that can embrace and take care of our anger. The second zone of energy is the energy of mindfulness. Mindfulness is the energy of the Buddha. It is available to us, and we are capable of generating it through mindful breathing and mindful walking. The Buddha within is not a mere concept. The Buddha within is not a theory or a notion. It is a reality, because all of us are capable of generating the energy of mindfulness.

Mindfulness means to be present, to be aware of what is going on. This energy is very crucial for the practice. The energy of mindfulness is like a big brother, big sister, or a mother, holding the younger one in her arms, taking good care of the suffering baby, which is our anger, despair, or jealousy.

Energy Zone One is anger, and Energy Zone Two is mindfulness. The practice is to use the energy of mindfulness to recognize and embrace the energy of anger. You have to do it tenderly, without violence. This is not an act of suppressing our anger. Mindfulness is you and anger is also you, so you shouldn't transform yourself into a battlefield, one side fighting the other. You should not believe that mindfulness is good and correct, while anger is evil and wrong. You should not think like that. You only need to recognize that anger is a negative energy and that mindfulness is a positive one. Then you can use the positive energy in order to take care of the negative one.

TRANSFORMATION

Organic Feelings

Our practice is based on the insight of non-duality. Both our negative feelings and positive feelings are organic and belong to the same reality. So there is no need to fight; we only need to embrace and take care. Therefore, in the Buddhist tradition, meditation does not mean you transform yourself into a battlefield, with the good fighting the evil. This is very important. You may think that you have to combat evil and chase it out of your heart and mind. But this is wrong. The practice is to transform yourself. If you don't have garbage, you have nothing to use in order to make compost. And if you have no compost, you have nothing to nourish the flower in you. You need the suffering, the afflictions in you. Since they are organic, you know that you can transform them and make good use of them.

The Insight of Inter-Being

Our method of practice should be non-violent. Non-violence can be born only from the insight of non-duality, of inter-being. This is the insight that everything is interconnected and nothing can exist by itself alone. Doing violence to others is doing violence to yourself. If you do not have the insight of non-duality, you will still be violent. You will still want to punish, to suppress, and to destroy. But once you have penetrated the reality of non-duality, you will smile at both the flower and garbage in you, you will embrace both. This insight is the ground for your non-violent action.

When you have the insight of non-duality and inter-being, you take care of your body in the most non-violent way possible. You take care of your mental formations, including your anger, with non-violence. You take care of your brother, your sister, your father, your mother, your community, and your society, with utmost tenderness. No violence can be born from this kind of attitude. You won't regard anyone as an enemy when you have penetrated the reality of inter-being.

The foundation of our practice is the insight of non-duality, the insight of non-violence. This insight teaches us how to treat our body with tenderness. We must treat our anger and our despair with tenderness. Anger has roots in non-anger elements. It has roots in the way we live our daily life. If we take good care of everything in us, without discrimination, we prevent our negative energies from dominating. We reduce the strength of our negative seeds so that they won't overwhelm us.

Expressing Anger Wisely

When anger manifests in us, we must recognize and accept that anger is there and that it needs to be tended to. At this moment we are advised not to say anything, not to do anything out of anger. We immediately return to ourselves and invite the energy of mindfulness to manifest also, in order to embrace, recognize, and take good care of our anger.

But we are advised to tell the other person that we are angry, that we suffer. "Darling, I suffer, I'm angry, and I want you to know it." Then if you are a good practitioner, you also add, "I'm doing my best to take care of my anger." And you can conclude with the third sentence, "Please, do help me," because he or she is still very intimate, very close to you. You still need him or her. Expressing your anger in this way is extremely wise. It is very truthful, very faithful because in the beginning of your relationship, you made a vow with your partner that you would share everything, positive or negative.

This kind of language, this kind of communication will inspire respect, and motivate the other person to look back and to practice like you. He or she will see that you respect yourself. You demonstrate that when you are angry, you know how to take care of your anger. You are doing your best in order to embrace it, and so you no longer consider your partner as an enemy to be punished. You see him or her as an ally who is still there to support you. These three sentences are very positive things to say.

Remember that you have to tell him or her within twenty-four hours. The Buddha said that a monk has the right to be angry, but not for more than one night. It's not healthy to keep your anger inside for too long. Do not keep your suffering or your anger to yourself for more than one day. You have to say these three things in a calm, loving way, and you must train yourself to do so. If you are not calm enough to express your anger and the deadline is drawing close, then you have to write the three sentences down on a piece of paper and deliver it to him or her. "Darling, I am angry, I suffer. I don't know why you have done this to me, why you have said this to me. I want you to know that I suffer. I am doing my best to practice taking care of my anger. Darling, I need you to help me." You have to deliver this kind of peace note to him and make sure that he will get it. The moment you tell him or deliver the note to him, you will already feel some relief.

TRANSFORMATION

An Appointment for Friday Evening

You may like to add something to your three sentences, to your peace note: "Let us sit down Friday evening and look deeply together." Perhaps you say this on Monday or Tuesday, so you still have another three or four days to practice. During this time, both of you will have a chance to look back and understand better what caused the conflict. You can come together any time, but Friday evening is good because if you can reconcile, if you can sort it out, then you will have a wonderful weekend together.

Until Friday evening comes, you practice mindful breathing and looking deeply to understand the roots of your anger. Whether you are driving, walking, cooking, or washing, you continue to embrace your anger with mindfulness. By doing so, you have a chance to look deeply into the nature of your anger. You discover that the main cause of your suffering is the seed of anger in you, because it has been watered too often, by yourself and by other people.

Anger is in us in the form of a seed. The seeds of love and compassion are also there. In our consciousness, there are many negative seeds and also many positive seeds. The practice is to avoid watering the negative seeds, and to identify and water the positive seeds every day. This is the practice of love.

Selective Watering

You have to protect yourself and your beloved ones by practicing selective watering. You say, "Darling, if you really care for
me, if you really love me, please do not water the negative seeds
in me every day. If you do, I'll be very unhappy, and if I'm unhappy, I'll make you unhappy. So please, please don't water the
seeds of anger, intolerance, irritation, or despair in me. And I
promise not to water these seeds in you. I know that you also
have negative seeds, and I'll be very careful not to water these
seeds in you, because I know if I do, you'll be very unhappy.
And then I will suffer also. I vow only to water the positive seeds
in you—the seeds of love, compassion, and understanding."

In Plum Village, we call this the practice of selective watering. If you get angry very easily, it is because your seed of
anger has been watered frequently over many years. You have
allowed it to be watered. You have not signed a contract with
the people around you, agreeing to water only the good seeds.
You have not practiced protecting yourself. If you don't protect yourself, you don't protect those you love.

When we embrace anger and take good care of our anger,
we obtain relief. We can look deeply into it and gain many in-
sights. The first insight may be that the seed of anger in us
has grown a little too big, and it is the main cause of our mis-

ery. As we begin to see this fact, we realize that the other person is only a secondary cause. The other person is not the main cause of our anger.

If we continue to look deeply, we see that the other person suffers a great deal. Someone who suffers a lot always makes the people around him or her suffer. He does not know how to manage his suffering, how to embrace and transform it. So his suffering continues to grow every day. In the past, we have not helped him. We have not practiced selective watering. If we had practiced watering the positive seeds in him every day, he would not be the way he is today.

The practice of selective watering is very effective. Just one hour of practice can make a big difference. One hour of watering the flower in the other person can make him or her begin to bloom. It is not so difficult to do.

Flower Watering

Some years ago, a couple from Bordeaux came to Plum Village to attend a dharma talk. We were celebrating the Buddha's birthday, and I was giving a talk on selective watering, flower watering. I noticed that the wife was crying silently during the dharma talk. Afterwards, I approached the husband and said, "Your flower needs to be watered." He understood immediately what I meant and on the way back home, he began to water his wife's positive seeds. The journey took only one hour and ten minutes. When they arrived home, the children were very surprised to see their mother so fresh and happy, because she had not been like that for a long time.

She had many wonderful seeds in her, but her husband had not recognized them. He had not watered them. He had watered only her negative seeds because he did not practice. It's not that he was unable to water the positive seeds in her. He was very capable of flower watering, but he needed to come to Plum Village and be reminded of this practice. He needed his teacher to urge him to do it. This is why having a community of practice is so important. You need the sangha; you need a brother, sister, or friend to remind you of what you already know. The dharma is in you, but it also needs to be watered, in order to manifest and become a reality. If you had really practiced watering the positive seeds in your beloved, then he or she would not cause you so much suffering today. So you are partly responsible for your suffering.

Going Back to Help

Until your appointment on Friday, practice looking deeply in order to identify your part in the conflict. Don't blame everything on the other person. Recognize first that the main cause of your suffering is the seed of anger in you, and that the other person is only a secondary cause.

When you begin to understand your role in the conflict, you feel even more relieved. Because you are capable of breathing mindfully, of embracing your anger, and releasing your negative energy, you feel much better after fifteen minutes of practice.

But the other person may still be in hell. She may still be suffering a lot. Your beloved one is your flower, you are responsible for her. You have made a vow to take care of him. You know you are also partly responsible for the way he or she is now because you have not practiced, you have not taken care of your flower. You feel compassion for her and suddenly you are motivated by the desire to go back and help her. The other person may be someone very dear to you. If you don't help, who will?

The moment you are motivated by the desire to return to the other and help, you know that all the energy of anger has been transformed into the energy of compassion. Your practice has born fruit. The compost, the garbage, has been transformed back into a flower. It may take fifteen minutes, half an hour, or one hour. It depends on your level of concentration, your level of mindfulness. It depends on the amount of wisdom and insight you gain during your practice.

It may be only Tuesday and you still have three days before your scheduled meeting on Friday. You don't want the other person to worry and to suffer anymore. So after you have identified your responsibility, you immediately pick up the phone and call him. "Darling, I feel much, much better right now. I have been the victim of a wrong perception. I see clearly how I caused both of us to suffer. Please don't worry about Friday night." You do this out of love.

Most of the time, anger is born from a wrong perception. If, when looking into the cause of your suffering, you find out that your anger was born from a wrong perception, you have to tell the other person right away. He didn't want to make you suffer, he didn't want to destroy you, but somehow you believed he did. Every one of us must practice looking deeply into our perceptions, whether we are a father, mother, child, or partner.

Are You Sure You're Right?

A man once had to leave home for a long time. Before he left, his wife got pregnant, but he didn't know it. When he returned, his wife had given birth to a child. He suspected that the little boy was not his, and believed that he was the son of a neighbor who used to come and work for the family. He looked at the little boy with suspicion. He hated him. He saw the neighbor's face in the little boy's face. Then one day the man's brother came to visit for the first time. When he saw the little boy, he said to the father, "He looks just like you. He's your exact duplicate." The brother's visit was a happy event, because it helped the father to get rid of his wrong perception. But the wrong perception had controlled this man's life for twelve years. It made the father suffer deeply. It made his wife suffer deeply, and, of course, the little boy suffered from that kind of hatred.

We act on the basis of wrong perceptions all the time. We should not be sure of any perception we have. When you look at the beautiful sunset, you may be quite sure that you are seeing the sun as it is in that moment, but a scientist will tell you that the image of the sun that you see is the image of the sun from eight minutes ago. Sunlight takes eight minutes to reach the earth from such a long distance. Also, when you see a star, you think that the star is there, but the star may have disappeared already, one, two, or ten thousand years before.

We have to be very careful with our perceptions, otherwise we will suffer. It is very helpful to write on a piece of paper, "Are you sure?" and hang it up in your room. In medical clinics and hospitals, they are beginning to hang up these kinds of signs: "Even if you are sure, check again." It is a caution that if a disease is not detected early, then it will be very difficult to heal. The medical doctors are not thinking in terms of mental formations. They are thinking in terms of a hidden disease. But we can also make use of this slogan—"Even if you are sure, check again." We have made ourselves suffer, we made a hell for ourselves and our beloved ones because of our perceptions. Are you sure of your perception?

There are people who suffer from a wrong perception for ten or twenty years. They are sure the other person has betrayed them or hates them, even though the other person has only good intentions. A person who is the victim of a wrong perception makes himself and the people around him suffer a lot.

When you are angry, and you suffer, please go back and inspect very deeply the content, the nature of your perceptions. If you are capable of removing the wrong perception, peace and happiness will be restored in you, and you will be able to love the other person again.

Looking Into Anger Together

When the other person knows that you are doing your best, looking into the cause of your anger, she also is motivated to practice. While driving, while cooking, she will ask herself, "What have I done? What have I said to make him suffer that much?" And she also will have a chance to practice looking deeply. She knows that in the past, she has reacted in ways that made you suffer. She begins to question her belief that she is not responsible for your suffering. If she finds out that she was unskillful when saying or doing something, then she has to call or fax you to tell you that she is sorry.

So if both of you get some insight during the week, you don't need to wait for Friday. Friday evening can then become a very joyful time when both of you sit together and enjoy a nice meal, or perhaps a cup of tea and a piece of cake. You can celebrate your love and your relationship.

Sharing Everything, Even When It's Difficult

If neither of you has succeeded in the practice, then Friday is a time for you to practice deep listening and loving speech. The one who is angry has the right to tell the other what is in his heart. If it is your partner who is angry, you just listen, because you have made the promise to listen and not to react. You do your best to practice compassionate listening. You listen not for the purpose of judging, criticizing, or analyzing. You listen only to help the other person to express himself and find some relief from his suffering.

When you share your suffering, you have the right to say everything in your heart—it is your duty to do so, because the other person has the right to know everything. You have made a commitment to each other. You should tell him everything that is in your heart, with only one condition—you must use calm and loving speech. The moment irritation manifests, the moment you think that you are going to lose your calm, your serenity, please stop. "Darling, I cannot continue now, may we meet another time? I need to practice more mindful walking and breathing. I'm not at my best right now, so I do not think I can succeed in the practice of loving speech." The other person will agree to postpone the session until later, perhaps next Friday.

If you are the one who listens, you also practice mindful breathing. Practice mindful breathing to empty yourself of any ideas or notions, in order to listen. Listen with compassion, and be there with your whole being to give the other person relief. You do have the seed of compassion within you, and it will manifest when you see that the other person suffers so much. Therefore you vow to be the Bodhisattva, the Great Being of deep listening. This Bodhisattva of Great Compassion must be a real person, and not just an idea.

With Compassion You Don't Make Mistakes

You can make a mistake only when you forget that the other person suffers. You tend to believe that you are the only one who suffers, and that the other person is enjoying your suffering. You will say and do mean and cruel things when you believe that you are the only one who suffers and that the other person does not suffer at all. The awareness that the other person suffers very much will help you to play the role of the Bodhisattva of deep listening. Compassion becomes possible, and you can keep compassion alive during the whole time of listening. You'll be the best therapist for him or her.

During the time the other person speaks, he may be very judgmental, only blaming and punishing. He may be very bitter and cynical. Yet, because compassion is still in you, this does not affect you. The nectar of compassion is so wonderful. If you are committed to keeping it alive, then you are protected. What the other person says will not touch off the anger and irritation in you, because compassion is the real antidote for anger. Nothing can heal anger except compassion. This is why the practice of compassion is a very wonderful practice.

Compassion is possible only when understanding is there. Understanding what? Understanding that the other person suffers and that I must help. If I don't help, who is going to help? When listening, you may notice a lot of wrong perceptions in the other person's speech. Still, you remain compassionate, because you know she is a victim of wrong perception. If you try to correct her, you may cut her off, preventing her from speaking out and fully expressing herself. So just sit and listen with all your attention, with your best intentions, and this will be very healing.

If you want to help correct her wrong perception, you have to wait until the moment is right. While listening, your only aim is to give her a chance to speak out and share what is in her heart. You don't say anything. This Friday evening is entirely for her to speak. You just listen. Then, perhaps a few days later, when she feels much better, you try to give her the information that she needs to correct her perception. "Darling, the other day you said something, but that is not really what happened. What happened is . . ." Use loving speech when you correct her. If necessary, ask a friend who knows what really happened to help the other person understand the true situation so that she can be freed from her wrong perceptions.

Patience Is the Mark of True Love

Anger is a living thing. It comes up, and it needs time to go back down. Even if you have clear evidence to convince someone that his anger is entirely based on a wrong perception, please don't interfere right away. Like craving, jealousy, and all afflictions, anger needs time to die down. This is the case even after the other person realizes that he or she misunderstood the situation. When you turn off a fan, it continues to spin a few thousand times before stopping. Anger is like that. Don't expect the other person to stop being angry right away. That's not realistic. You have to allow anger to die down slowly. So don't rush.

Patience is the mark of true love. A father has to be patient in order to show his love for his son or daughter. A mother, a son, and a daughter also. If you want to love, you must learn to be patient. If you are not patient, you cannot help the other person.

You must also be patient with yourself. The practice of embracing your anger takes time. But just five minutes of mindful breathing, mindful walking, and embracing your anger can be effective. If five minutes is not enough, take ten minutes, and if ten minutes is not enough, take fifteen minutes. Give yourself as much time as you need. The practices of mindful breathing and mindful walking outdoors are wonderful ways to embrace your anger. Even the practice of jogging is very helpful. Just like when you cook potatoes, you need to keep the fire going for at least fifteen or twenty minutes. You cannot eat raw potatoes. You have to cook your anger on the fire of mindfulness. It may take ten or twenty minutes. It may take more.

Gaining a Victory

While cooking your potatoes, you have to cover the pot in order to prevent heat from escaping. That is concentration. So while you practice walking or breathing to take care of your anger, don't do anything else. Don't listen to the radio, don't watch television, don't read a book. Cover the pot and just do one thing. Just practice deep walking meditation, deep mindful breathing, and use one hundred percent of yourself in order to embrace your anger, exactly like you would take good care of a baby.

After some time of embracing and looking deeply, insight will come and your anger will diminish. You'll feel much better, and you'll be motivated to go back and help the other person. When you remove the lid of the pot, the potatoes will smell wonderful. Your anger will have been transformed into the energy of loving-kindness.

This is possible. It is like the tulips. When the energy of the sun is strong enough, the tulip has to open herself and show her heart to the sun. Your anger is a kind of flower. You have to embrace it with the sunshine of mindfulness. Let the energy of mindfulness penetrate into the energy of anger. After five or ten minutes of mindfulness, your anger will be transformed.

Every mental formation—anger, jealousy, despair, etc.—is sensitive to mindfulness the way all vegetation is sensitive to sunshine. By cultivating the energy of mindfulness, you can heal your body and your consciousness, because mindfulness is the energy of the Buddha. In Christianity, it is said that Jesus has the energy of God, of the Holy Spirit, within him. That is why he is able to heal many people. His healing energy is called the Holy Spirit. In Buddhist language, that energy is the energy of the Buddha, the energy of mindfulness.

Mindfulness contains the energy of concentration, understanding, and compassion. Thus, the practice of Buddhist meditation is the practice of generating the energy that will offer us concentration, compassion, understanding, love, and happiness. Everyone in a practice center is doing just that, so together we offer a powerful, collective zone of energy that embraces and protects us and the people who come to stay with us.

Even after one session of practice, we notice that we are very capable of taking care of our anger. We have gained a victory for ourselves and for our beloved ones. When we lose, we and our beloved ones lose. But when we win a victory, we win for the other person as well. So, even if the other person does not know the practice, we can practice for both ourselves and him or her. Don't wait for the other person to practice in order to start practicing. You can do it for both of you.

FIVE

COMPASSIONATE COMMUNICATION

There may have been a time when you could not communicate with your parents. Although you lived in the same house, you might have felt that your father or mother was very distant. In this situation, both parent and child suffer. Each side believes that there is only misunderstanding, hatred, and separation. The parent and child do not know that they have many things in common. They do not know that they both have the capacity to understand, to forgive, and to love each other. Therefore, it is very important to recognize the positive elements that are always there in us to prevent anger and other negative elements from dominating us.

The Sunshine Behind the Clouds

When it is raining, we think that there is no sunshine. But if we fly high in an airplane and go through the clouds, we rediscover the sunshine again. We see that the sunshine is always there. In a time of anger or despair, our love is still there also. Our capacity to communicate, to forgive, to be compassionate is still there. You have to believe this. We are more than our anger, we are more than our suffering. We must recognize that we do have within us the capacity to love, to understand, to be compassionate. If you know this, then when it rains you won't be desperate. You know that the rain is there, but the sunshine is still there somewhere. Soon the rain will stop, and the sun will shine again. Have hope. If you can remind yourself that the positive elements are still present within you and the other person, you will know that it is possible to break through, so that the best things in both of you can come up and manifest again.

The practice is there for that. The practice will help you touch the sunshine, touch the Buddha, the goodness within you so that you can transform the situation. You can call this goodness anything you want to, whatever is familiar to you from your own spiritual tradition.

Deep down you must know that you are capable of being

peace. Develop the conviction that the energy of the Buddha is in you. The only thing you need to do is to call on it for help. You can do this by practicing mindful breathing, mindful walking, and mindful sitting.

Training Ourselves to Listen Deeply

Communicating is a practice. You have to be skillful in order to communicate. Good will is not enough. You have to learn how to do it. Maybe you have lost your capacity to listen. Maybe the other person has spoken so often with bitterness, always condemning and blaming, that you have had enough. You cannot listen anymore. You begin to try to avoid him or her. You don't have the capacity to listen to that person anymore.

You try to avoid him out of fear. You don't want to suffer. But this can also create a misunderstanding, and make him feel that you despise him. This can cause him a lot of suffering. You give him the impression that you want to boycott him, to ignore his presence. You cannot face him and at the same time you cannot avoid him. The only solution is to train yourself to be able to communicate again. Deep listening is the way.

We know that many people suffer, feeling that no one is

able to understand them or their situation. Everyone is too busy and no one seems to have the capacity to listen. But all of us need someone who can listen to us.

Today there are people who practice psychotherapy and they are supposed to be there for you, to sit and listen to you so that you can open your heart. They have to listen deeply in order to be real therapists. Real therapists have the capacity to listen with all their being, without prejudices, without judgment.

I don't know how therapists train themselves to acquire this kind of capacity to listen. A therapist also may be full of suffering. While sitting and listening to the client, the seeds of suffering in him or her may be watered. If the therapist is overwhelmed by his own suffering, how can he listen properly to the other person? When you are trained to be a therapist, you have to learn the art of deep listening.

Listening with empathy means you listen in such a way that the other person feels you are really listening, really understanding, hearing with your whole being—with your heart. But how many of us can listen like that? We agree in principle that we should listen with our heart, so that we can really hear what the other is saying. We agree that we should give the speaker the feeling that he is being listened to and being understood. Only that can give him a feeling of relief. But, in fact, how many of us can listen like that?

Listening to Give Relief

Deep listening, compassionate listening is not listening with the purpose of analyzing or even uncovering what has happened in the past. You listen first of all in order to give the other person relief, a chance to speak out, to feel that someone finally understands him or her. Deep listening is the kind of listening that helps us to keep compassion alive while the other speaks, which may be for half an hour or forty-five minutes. During this time you have in mind only one idea, one desire: to listen in order to give the other person the chance to speak out and suffer less. This is your only purpose. Other things like analyzing, understanding the past, can be a by-product of this work. But first of all listen with compassion.

Compassion Is the Antidote for Anger and Bitterness

If you keep compassion alive in you while listening, then anger and irritation cannot arise. Otherwise the things he says, the things she says will touch off your irritation, anger, and suffering. Compassion alone can protect you from becoming irritated, angry, or full of despair.

So you want to act as a Great Being while listening because you know that the other person suffers so much and needs you to step in and rescue him. But you have to be equipped with something to do the job.

When firemen come to help put out a fire, they have to have the right equipment. They must have ladders, water, and the kind of clothing that can protect them from fire. They have to know many ways to protect themselves and to put the fire out. When you listen deeply to someone who suffers, you step into a zone of fire. There is a fire of suffering, of anger burning in the person you are listening to. If you are not well equipped, you cannot help and you might become a victim of the fire in the other person. This is why you need equipment.

Your equipment here is compassion, which can be nourished and kept alive with the practice of mindful breathing. Mindful breathing generates the energy of mindfulness. Mindful breathing keeps your basic desire alive, the desire to help the other person speak out. When the other person speaks, his words might be full of bitterness, condemnation, and judgment. These words might touch off suffering in you. But if compassion is kept alive in you, through the practice of mindful breathing, you are protected. You are capable of sitting there and listening for one hour without suffering. Your compassion will nourish you, knowing that you are helping the other person to suffer less. Play the role of a Bodhisattva. You will be the best kind of therapist.

Compassion is born from happiness and also from understanding. When compassion and understanding are kept alive, you are safe. What the other person says will not make you suffer and you can listen deeply. You really listen. When you do not have the capacity to listen with compassion, you cannot just pretend you are listening. The other person will realize that you are full of ideas about suffering, but don't really understand him or her. When you have understanding, you can listen with compassion, you can listen deeply, and the quality of this listening is the fruit of your practice.

Nourishing Ourselves

Touching suffering can help us nourish our compassion and be able to recognize happiness when it is there. If we are not in contact with pain, we cannot know what real happiness is. So touching suffering is our practice. But each one of us has limits. We cannot do more than we can do.

This is why we have to take good care of ourselves. If you listen too much to the suffering, the anger of other people, you will be affected. You will be in touch only with suffering, and you won't have the opportunity to be in touch with other, positive elements. This will destroy your balance. Therefore, in your daily life, you have to practice so that you can be in touch with elements that do not constantly express suffering: the sky, the birds, the trees, the flowers, children—whatever is refreshing, healing, and nourishing in us and around us.

Sometimes you get lost in your suffering, in your worries. Let your friends rescue you. They may say, "Look how beautiful the sky is this morning. It is foggy, but it's really beautiful. Paradise is right here. Why don't you come back to the present and witness this beauty?" You are with the community, with brothers and sisters who are capable of being happy. So the community rescues you and helps you to be in touch again with the positive elements of life. This is the practice of nourishment. It's very important.

We should be able to live each day deeply, with joy, peace, and compassion because time goes by so quickly. Each morning I offer a stick of incense to the Buddha. I promise myself that I will enjoy every minute of the day that is given me to live. It is thanks to the practice of mindful walking and mindful breathing that I can enjoy deeply every moment of my daily life. Mindful breathing and mindful walking are like two friends, always helping me to delve into the here and the now and touch the wonders of life that are available.

We need to receive the nourishment we deserve. Listening to the sound of the bell is a very nourishing and pleasant practice. In Plum Village, whenever the phone rings, the clock chimes, or the monastery bell is invited, we have a chance to stop whatever we are doing, to stop our talking and our thinking. These are bells of mindfulness. When we hear the sound of the bell, we relax our body and return to our breathing. We realize that we are alive and can get in touch with many wonders of life that are present for us. We stop naturally, with enjoyment, not with solemnity or stiffness. Breathing in and out three times, we enjoy the fact that we are alive. When we stop, we restore our calm and peace, we become free. Our work becomes more enjoyable, and the people around us become more real.

The practice of stopping and breathing with the bell is an example of the kind of practice that helps you get in touch with the beautiful and nourishing elements in daily life. You can do it alone, but with the sangha you can do it much more easily. The community is always there. When you get lost in your suffering, it can rescue you and put you in touch with the positive elements of life.

To know our limits is our practice. Even if you are a spiritual teacher and you have the capacity of listening to people's suffering, you have to know your limits. You have to enjoy walking meditation. You have to enjoy your tea. You have to enjoy the company of happy people so that you get sufficient nourishment. To listen to the other person, you have to take care of yourself. On the one hand, you need to get the right nourishment every day. On the other hand, you need to practice nourishing compassion in yourself so that you can be well equipped for the task of listening. You have to play the role of a Great Being, someone who has so much happiness that she is able to rescue people from their suffering.

You Are Your Children

As a father or mother, you have to listen to your son or your daughter. This is very important because your son is yourself; your daughter is yourself. Your child is your continuation. The most important task for you is to restore communication between you and your child. If your heart does not function well, if your stomach is not in good health, you don't think of cutting it out and throwing it away. You cannot say, "You are not my heart! My heart does not behave like that. You are not my stomach! My stomach does not behave like that. I will have nothing to do with you anymore!" This is not intelligent. You might talk to your son or your daughter like that, and this is not intelligent, either.

The moment your son or daughter is conceived in your womb, you see yourself and the fetus as one. You may even begin to have a conversation with the baby, "Keep still my beloved one. I know you are there." You speak to him or to her with love. You become aware of what you consume, because whatever you eat and drink, the baby also eats and drinks. Your worries and your joy are the worries and joy of your baby. You and the baby are one.

When you give birth to the baby and the umbilical cord is cut, this awareness of your unity may begin to fade away. By the time your son or your daughter turns twelve or thirteen, you have completely forgotten that she or he is you. You think of him or her as a separate entity. You have problems with each other. Having a problem with your child is like having trouble with your stomach, your heart, your kidneys. If you believe that he is another person, a separate entity, you can say, "Go away! You are not my son! You are not my daughter! My son doesn't behave like that. My daughter doesn't behave like that." But because you cannot say this to your stomach or to your heart, you cannot say it to your son or your daughter. The Buddha said, "There is no separate self." You and your son, you and your daughter are just a continuation of many generations of ancestors. You are part of a long stream of life. Whatever your children do continues to affect you deeply—just like when they were in your womb. Whatever you do still affects your children deeply because they can never be cut off from you. Your happiness and suffering are your child's happiness and suffering and vice versa.

That is why you have to invest one hundred percent of yourself in the task of restoring communication.

Starting a Dialogue

Confusion and ignorance make us think that we are the only ones who suffer. We believe that our son or our daughter does not suffer. But in fact, whenever you suffer, your child also suffers. You are there in every cell of your son's body, in every cell of your daughter's body. Every emotion and every perception in your child, is your emotion and perception. Therefore we have to remember the insight that we had in the beginning that he and you, that she and you, are one. Start a dialogue with your son or your daughter.

In the past you have made mistakes. You have caused your stomach to suffer. The way you have eaten and drunk, the way you have worried has had a big impact on your stomach, your intestines, your heart. You are responsible for your heart, your intestines, and your stomach. In very much the same way, you are responsible for your son and your daughter. You cannot say that you are not responsible. It would be much wiser to come to your child and say, "My dear child, I know you suffer a lot. For many years, you have suffered a lot. When you suffer, I suffer, too. How can I be happy when my child suffers? So I recognize that both you and I suffer. Can we do something about it? Can we come together and search for a solution? Can we talk? I really want to restore communication, but alone, I cannot do much. I need your help."

If, as a father or mother, you are capable of saying things like this to your child, the situation may change because you know how to use loving speech. Your language comes from love, from understanding, and from enlightenment. Enlightenment of the fact that you and your child are one, and that happiness and well-being are not an individual matter. These concern both of you. So what you say to your child has to come from your love and understanding, the understanding that there is no separate self. You can speak like this because you understand the true nature of both yourself and your child. You know that your daughter is the way she is because you are the way you are. You are interdependent. You are the way you are because your son is the way he is. You are not separate.

Train yourself in the art of mindful living. Train yourself so that you can become skillful enough to restore communication. "My dear son, I know that you are me. You are my continuation, and when you suffer there is no way that I can be happy, so let us come together and sort things out. Please help me." The son also can learn to speak this way because he understands that if his father suffers, he cannot be happy either. Through the practice of mindfulness, the son can touch the reality of no separate self and can learn to restore communication with his father. He may be the one who takes the initiative.

The same thing can happen between partners. You have vowed to live as one. With deep sincerity you have vowed to share your happiness and suffering. Telling your partner that you need his or her help to begin anew is only a continuation of those vows. Every one of us has the capacity for talking and listening like this.

Love Letters

There is a French woman who kept old love letters from her husband. He wrote her beautiful letters before they married. Every time she got a letter from him, she savored every sentence—every word—it was so sweet, so understanding, so full of love. She was delighted whenever she got a letter, so she kept all his letters in a biscuit box. One morning, while she was rearranging her closet, she discovered the ancient biscuit box where she stored all his letters. It had been a long time since she had seen it. The box of letters told of the most wonderful time, when she and her husband were young, when they loved each other and believed that without each other they could not survive.

But in the past several years, both husband and wife had suffered a lot. They didn't enjoy looking at each other anymore. They didn't enjoy talking to each other anymore. They didn't write letters to each other anymore. The day before she found the box, her husband informed her that he had to go on a business trip. He did not find it pleasant to stay home, and perhaps he was looking for a little bit of happiness or pleasure on his trips. She was aware of that. When her husband told her that he had to go to New York for a meeting, she said, "If you have work to do, please go ahead." She had grown used to this, it was very ordinary. Then, instead of returning home as planned, he telephoned and said, "I have to stay two more days, because there are things I still need to do." She accepted this very easily, because even when he was at home, she was not happy.

After hanging up, she began to rearrange her closet and she discovered the box. It was a box of "Lu" biscuits—a very famous brand in France. She was curious because it had been a long time since she opened that box. She put down her duster, opened the box, and smelled something very familiar. She took out one of the letters and she stood there and read it. How sweet was the letter! His language was full of understanding and love. She felt very refreshed, like a piece of dry land finally exposed to the rain. She opened another letter to read because it was so wonderful. Finally she brought the whole box of letters to the table, sat down, and read one after another until she finished all forty-six or forty-seven of them. The seeds of her past happiness were still there. They had been buried under many layers of suffering—but they were still there. So while reading that letter he wrote when he was young, and full of love, she felt the seeds of happiness in her begin to be watered.

When you do something like this, you water the seeds of happiness that lie deep within your consciousness. In the recent past, her husband had not been using that kind of language at all. But now, when reading the letters, she could hear her husband speaking in that sweet way. Happiness had been a reality for them. Why did they now live in a kind of hell? She could hardly remember that he used to talk to her like that, but it had been a reality. He was able to talk to her in that kind of language.

Watering the Seeds of Happiness

During the hour and a half she spent reading all these letters, she watered the seeds of happiness in herself. She realized that both of them had been unskillful. They had watered the seeds of suffering in each other, and they had not been able to water the seeds of happiness. After reading all the letters, she was motivated by the desire to sit down and write him a letter to tell him how happy she was at that time, in the beginning of their relationship. She wrote that she wished the happiness of those golden years could be rediscovered and re-created. And now she could again call him, "My beloved one," with all honesty and sincerity.

She spent forty-five minutes writing that letter. It was a real love letter—addressed to the charming young man who had written the letters she kept in a box. Reading his letters and then writing a letter took about three hours. It was a time of practice, but she did not know she was practicing. After having written the letter, she felt very light inside. The letter had not yet been delivered; her husband had not yet read it; but she felt much better because the seeds of happiness had been reawakened, they had been watered. She went upstairs and put the letter on his desk. And for the rest of the day, she was happy. She was happy just because the letters had watered the positive seeds in her.

While reading the letters and writing to her husband, she gained some insight. Neither of them had been skillful. Neither of them knew how to preserve the happiness they deserved. In their speech, in their actions, they created hell for each other. Both accepted living as a family, as a couple, but they no longer had any happiness. After having understood this, she was confident that if both of them tried to practice, happiness could be restored. She became full of hope and no longer suffered as she had in the past years.

When her husband came home, he went upstairs, and he saw the letter on his desk. In the letter, she wrote: "I'm partly responsible for our suffering, for the fact that we don't have the happiness that both of us deserve. Let us begin anew and restore communication. Let us make peace, harmony, and happiness a reality again." He spent a lot of time reading the letter and looking deeply into what she had written. He did not know that he was practicing meditation. But he was practicing also, because by reading his wife's letter, the seeds of happiness in him were also watered. He stayed upstairs for a long time, looking deeply and getting the same insight that she had gotten the day before. Because of that, both of them had a chance to begin anew and to restore their happiness.

Nowadays, people, lovers, don't write letters to each other anymore. They just pick up the phone and say, "Are you free tonight? Shall we go out?" That's all, and you have nothing to keep. That is a pity. We must learn to write love letters again. Write to your beloved one, he may be your father or your son. She may be your daughter, your mother, your sister, or your friend. Take time to write down your gratitude and love.

Small Miracles

There are many ways you can restore communication. If you find it too difficult to talk to your son, why don't you practice mindful walking and mindful breathing for one or two days? Then sit down and write him a love letter. You can use the same kind of language: "My dear son, I know that you have suffered terribly, and as your father, I am partly responsible because I didn't know how to transmit the best of myself to you. I know you have not been able to communicate your suffering to me, and I want this to change. I want to be there for you. Let us help each other and try to improve our communication." You have to learn to speak this kind of language.

Loving speech will rescue us. Compassionate listening will rescue us. This is a miracle performed by us, as practitioners. You have the capacity to do it. You have enough peace, enough compassion and understanding in the depth of your consciousness. You have to call on it for help, call on the Buddha within. With a loving friend supporting you, it will be possible for you to begin anew and restore communication.

SIX

YOUR HEART SUTRA

Moment of Gratitude, Moment of Enlightenment

There are moments when we feel very grateful for the other person in our life. We deeply appreciate his or her presence. We are full of compassion, gratitude, and love. We have experienced moments like this in our life. We feel so grateful that the other person is still alive, that she is still with us, and has stood by our side during very difficult times. I would suggest that if such a moment happens again, take advantage of it.

To truly profit from this time, withdraw to a place where you can be alone with yourself. Don't just go to the other person and say, "I'm grateful you are there." That is not enough.

You can do this later. Right at that moment, it is better to withdraw into your room or to a quiet place, and immerse yourself in that feeling of gratitude. Then write down your feelings, your gratitude, your happiness. In half a page or one page, do your best to express yourself in writing, or record yourself on tape.

This moment of gratitude is a moment of enlightenment, of mindfulness, of intelligence. It is a manifestation from the depths of your consciousness. You have this understanding and insight in you. But when you get angry, your gratitude and love do not seem to be there at all. You feel as if they have never existed, so you have to write them down on a sheet of paper and keep it safely. From time to time, take it out and read it again.

The Heart Sutra, a scripture that is chanted daily by many Buddhists, is the essence of the Buddha's teachings on wisdom. What you have written is a Heart Sutra because it comes from your heart—not from the heart of a Bodhisattva or the Buddha, but from your own heart. It is *your* Heart Sutra.

Chant Your Heart Sutra Daily

We can all learn something from the story of the woman who was saved by the love letters she kept in a biscuit box.

When you read such letters from the heart, you are saved by them. Your savior doesn't come from outside; it comes from inside. You can love; you do have the capacity to appreciate the other person, to feel grateful. This is a blessing. You know you are lucky to have met your partner, you are lucky to have your beloved one in your life. Why do you let this truth fly away? It is in your heart. So you have to chant your Heart Sutra every day. You have to look at it. Every time you touch the love and appreciation in you, you feel grateful again, you cherish his or her presence again.

You have to be alone in order to fully appreciate the other person's presence. If you are always together, then you may begin to take him for granted, forgetting to enjoy his beauty and goodness. Every now and then, take three or seven days off. Take time away from him in order to be able to appreciate him more. Although you are far away from him, he is more real to you, more substantial than when you are constantly together. During the time you are apart, you will remember how important, how precious he is to you.

So, please, write or produce your own Heart Sutra, or sutras, and keep it in a sacred place. Try to chant your sutra often. Then, when anger overwhelms you, and you are not skillful enough to embrace it, your Heart Sutra will help tremendously. Pick it up, practice breathing deeply in and out, and read it. Right away you will come back to yourself, and you will suffer much less. When you read your Heart Sutra, you will know what to do and how to respond. The challenge is getting yourself to do it. You must create the conditions, prepare, plan, and organize, so that you can really profit from your intelligence. Use your talent to arrange and create these kinds of practices.

Leave the Shore of Anger

You are still standing on the shore of suffering and anger. Why don't you leave this shore, and go to the other shore— the shore of non-anger, peace, and liberation? It's much more pleasant there. Why do you have to spend several hours, one evening, or even days suffering in anger? There is a boat you can use to cross very quickly to the other shore. That boat is the practice of returning to ourselves, through mindful breathing, so that we can look deeply at our suffering, anger, and depression and smile at them. Doing this, we overcome our pain and cross over to the other shore.

Don't stay on this shore and continue to be the victim of your anger. Non-anger is in you; non-anger is possible. Just cross the river and go to the other shore, the shore of non-anger. It is cool, pleasant, and refreshing there. Don't allow yourself to be tyrannized by your anger. Free yourself, liberate yourself. Cross over with the help of a teacher, other friends who practice, and your own practice. Rely on these boats to cross the river and go to the other shore.

Right now you may be standing on the shore of confusion, anger, or doubt. Don't stay there; go to the other shore. With the sangha, your brothers and sisters in the dharma, your practice of walking and breathing, your practice of looking deeply, and of chanting your own Heart Sutra, you will cross very quickly. Maybe in just a few minutes. You have the right to be happy. You have the right to be compassionate, to be loving. The seed of awakening is in you. With the practice, you can turn this seed into a flower right away. You can end your suffering, because the dharma is immediately effective. It is quicker than aspirin.

Give a Gift When You Are Angry

There may be times when you are angry with someone, and you try everything you can to transform your anger, but nothing seems to work. In this case, the Buddha proposes that you give the other person a present. It sounds childish, but it is very effective. When we're angry with someone, we want to hurt them. Giving them a present changes that into wanting to make them happy. So, when you are angry with someone, send him a present. After you have sent it, you will stop being angry with him. It's very simple, and it always works.

Don't wait until you get angry to go and buy the present. When you feel very grateful, when you feel you love him or her so much, then go and buy the present right away. But don't send it; don't give it to the other person yet. Keep it. You may have the luxury of having two or three presents stored secretly in your drawer. Later, when you feel angry, take one out and deliver it. It is very effective. The Buddha was very smart.

The Relief of Understanding

When you are angry, you want to ease your suffering. That is a natural tendency. There are many ways to find relief, but the greatest relief comes from understanding. When understanding is there, anger will go away by itself. When you understand the situation of the other person, when you understand the nature of suffering, anger has to vanish, because it will be transformed into compassion.

Looking deeply is the medicine most recommended for anger. If you look, you will understand the other's difficulties and their deepest aspiration that they have never been able to realize. Then compassion is born in you and compassion is the antidote for anger. If you allow compassion to spring from your heart, the fire of anger will die right away.

Most of our suffering is born from our lack of understanding and insight that there is no separate self. The other person is you, you are the other person. If you get in touch with that truth, anger will vanish.

Compassion is a beautiful flower born of understanding. So when you get angry with someone, practice breathing in and out mindfully. Look deeply into the situation to see the true nature of your own and the other person's suffering, and you will be liberated.

Dangers of Venting

There are therapists who advise us to express our anger in order to feel better. They suggest we say or do things to let our anger out, like taking a stick and hitting a tire, or slamming the door with all your might. They also suggest hitting a pillow. These therapists believe that this is the way to remove the energy of anger in us. They call it "venting."

When you have smoke in your room, you want to ventilate the room so the smoke can escape. Anger is a kind of smoke, an energy that makes you suffer. When the smoke of anger comes up, you want to open a door and turn on the fan, so the anger will go out. So you ventilate by hitting a stone or a tree with a stick, or by pounding on your pillow. I have seen many people practice like that. Actually, they do get some temporary relief. But, the side effects of venting are very harmful. They will make you suffer much more.

Anger needs energy to manifest. When you try to vent it by using all your might to hit something or pound your pillow, half an hour later, you will be exhausted. Because you are exhausted, you will have no energy left to feed your anger. You may think that anger is no longer there, but that's not true; you are simply too tired to be angry.

It is the roots of anger in you that produce anger. The roots of anger lie in ignorance, wrong perceptions, in the lack of understanding and compassion. When you vent your anger, you simply open the energy that is feeding your anger. The roots of anger are always there, and by expressing anger like that, you are strengthening the roots of anger in yourself. That is the danger of venting.

There was an article in *The New York Times,* March 9, 1999, on anger, titled "Letting Out Aggression Is Called Bad Advice." According to this article, a lot of research has been done by social psychologists, and they concluded that trying to express your anger and your aggression by hitting a pillow and the like won't help at all. In fact, it will make the situation worse.

While you pound the pillow, you are not calming or reducing your anger—you are rehearsing it. If you practice hitting a pillow every day, then the seed of anger in you will grow every day. And someday, when you meet the person who made you angry, you may practice what you have learned. You will just hit the other person and end up in jail. That is why handling your aggression by hitting a pillow, or venting, is not helpful at all. It is dangerous. It is not truly ventilating the energy of anger since anger is not getting out of your system.

Venting your anger is a practice based on ignorance. When you imagine the object of your hate as a pillow, hitting the object of your hate, you rehearse your ignorance and anger. Instead of lessening your violence and anger, you become more violent and angry.

A number of therapists have confirmed that the practice of venting anger is dangerous. They told me that they stopped advising their clients to do it. After their clients vent by hitting pillows, they are tired, and so they think they feel better. But after they rest and have some food, if someone comes and waters the seed of anger in them, they become even angrier than before. They have fed the roots of their anger by rehearsing it.

When Mindfulness Is There, You Are Safe

We have to be there for our anger, we have to recognize its presence and take good care of it. In psychotherapy this is called "getting in touch with our anger." It is wonderful and very important. You have to recognize and embrace anger when it manifests instead of suppressing it.

But the important question here is who is the one getting in touch with, taking care of, and recognizing anger? Anger is an energy, and if that energy is overwhelming, you can be a victim of it. You should be able to generate another kind of energy that can recognize and take care of the anger. Anger is a zone of energy that needs to be touched, that needs to be recognized. The question is, what is touching what? What energy can do the touching and the recognizing? It is the energy of mindfulness. So every time we get angry, we practice mindful breathing and mindful walking, in order to touch the seed of mindfulness and generate the energy of mindfulness in us.

Mindfulness is not there to suppress. Mindfulness is there to welcome, to recognize: "Hello, my little anger, I know you are there. My old friend." Mindfulness is the energy that helps us to be aware of what is there. To be mindful is always to be mindful of something. You may be mindful of your in-breath, or out-breath, and that is mindfulness of breathing. You may be mindful of the tea you are drinking, and that is mindfulness of drinking. When you eat mindfully, that is mindfulness of eating. When you walk mindfully, it is mindfulness of walking.

In this case, we practice mindfulness of anger. "I'm aware that I'm angry, and I'm aware that anger is in me." So, mindfulness is touching, recognizing, greeting, and embracing. It does not fight or suppress. The role of mindfulness is like the role of a mother, embracing and soothing the suffering child. Anger is in you; anger is your baby, your child. You have to take very good care of it. When it recognizes anger, mindfulness says, "Hello there, my anger, I know you are there. I will take good care of you, don't worry." The moment mindfulness is there, you are safe, you can smile, because the energy of the Buddha is born in you.

If you don't know how to handle your anger, it can kill you. Without mindfulness, you may become the victim of anger. It can make you vomit blood and even die. Many people die because of anger—it is a shock to your whole system, it creates tremendous pressure and pain inside you. When the Buddha is present, when the energy of mindfulness is there, you are protected. Mindfulness helps you take care of your situation. When the big brother is there, the younger brother is safe. When the mother is there, the child is safe. Through the practice, the mother or the big brother in you becomes better and better at taking care of anger.

While recognizing and embracing our anger, we must generate mindfulness continuously. We can do this by the practice of continuous mindful walking and breathing. If you don't have mindfulness, nothing you do will bring you relief, even if you hit a pillow with all your might. Hitting a pillow doesn't help you get in touch with your anger or discover the nature of your anger. You don't even get in touch with the pillow. If you were in touch with the pillow, then you would know that it was only a pillow, and not your enemy. Why do you hit the pillow like that? Because you don't know that it is just a pillow.

When you really get in touch with something, then you will know its true nature. If you get in touch with one person deeply, then you know who she or he truly is. If mindfulness is not there, getting in touch with something or someone is not possible. Without mindfulness, you become a victim because your anger pushes you to do harmful things.

You Are the Object of Your Anger

Who do you think you are? You are the other person. If you get angry with your son, you are getting angry with yourself.

You are wrong to think that your son is not you. Your son is you. Genetically, physiologically, scientifically, your son is your continuation. That is the real truth. Who is your mother? Your mother is you. You are her continuation as a descendant, and she is your continuation as an ancestor. She links you to all those who came before, and you link her to all the future generations. You belong to the same stream of life. To think that she is a different entity, to think that you can have nothing to do with her is sheer ignorance. When a young man says, "I no longer want to have anything to do with my father," that is sheer ignorance, because the young man is nothing but his father.

As a mother, pregnant with your child, you had this insight, that your child is you. You ate for your baby, you drank for your baby, you took care of your baby. When you took care of yourself, you took care of your baby. You were very careful, because you knew that the baby was you. But by the time your child reaches the age of thirteen or fourteen, you begin to lose this insight. You and your child feel separated, less connected. You don't know how to improve your relationship, to make peace after a fight. Soon, the gap between the two of you grows bigger and more solid. Your relationship becomes very difficult and full of conflict.

Insight Stops Anger

It may seem like you are two separate entities, but if you look deeper, you will see that you are still one. So settling the dispute, restoring peace between you both, is like restoring peace within yourself, within your own body. You and your child are of the same nature, you belong to the same reality.

Many years ago when I was in London, I walked into a bookshop and saw a book entitled *My Mother, Myself.* This is an intelligent title. Your mother, yourself. You can write another book, *My Daughter, Myself.* Or *My Son, Myself; My Father, Myself.* It is the actual reality. When you get angry with your son, you are getting angry with yourself. When you punish your son, you punish yourself. When you inflict suffering on your father, you inflict suffering on yourself. We understand this when we have the insight of non-self, the insight that the self is made of non-self elements, like our father, mother, all our ancestors, as well as the sun, the air, and the earth.

When you can touch this insight, the reality of non-self, you know that happiness and suffering are not individual matters. Your suffering is the suffering of your beloved ones. Their happiness is your happiness. When you know this, you will not be tempted by the idea of punishing or of blaming. You'll behave with much more wisdom. This intelligence, this wisdom, is the fruit of your contemplation, of your looking deeply. So when you read your Heart Sutra, it helps you to remember the insight that your child, your partner, is you.

We read a sutra to immerse ourselves in the truth, in the insight of non-self. The Heart Sutra that you are encouraged to write is a sutra that comes from your own insight that you and the other person are one. *The Heart Sutra* is about wisdom. So is your Heart Sutra. It reminds you of the wisdom that you are not separate, isolated selves. It reminds you of the wisdom of your love. When you are angry, when you are misled by the idea that you are a separate self, reading that Heart Sutra will help you return to yourself again. When insight is there, then the Buddha is there, and you are safe. You don't have to suffer anymore.

We have to constantly remind ourselves that there are many ways of getting relief from anger, but the best, the deepest relief comes from understanding, the insight of non-self. Non-self is not an abstract philosophy. Non-self is a reality that you can touch by living mindfully. The insight of non-self will restore peace and harmony between you and the other person. You deserve peace, you deserve happiness. That is why you have to sit down with him, with her, and design a strategy for living together.

Furthermore, you yourself must also figure out a way of living that will bring you harmony and peace. You have to sign a peace treaty with yourself, because very often you are torn apart by the war and the conflict inside of you. You are at war because you lack wisdom, you lack insight. With understanding, you can restore peace and harmony in yourself and in your relationships with others. You will know how to act and how to react with intelligence so that you are no longer in a war zone, a zone of conflict. If there is peace and harmony in you, the other person will recognize it, and peace and harmony between both of you will be restored quickly. You will be much more pleasant, much easier to be with, and that will help the other person tremendously.

So to help your son, make peace with yourself. Look deeply into yourself. If you want to help your mother, restore peace in yourself. Discover the insight that will allow you to help your mother. Helping yourself is the first condition for helping the other. Let go of the illusion called self. This is the essence of the practice that will free you and the other person from anger and suffering.

SEVEN

NO ENEMIES

Begin with Yourself

Without communication, no real understanding can be possible. But be sure that you can communicate with yourself first. If you cannot communicate with yourself, how do you expect to communicate with another person? Love is the same. If you don't love yourself, you cannot love someone else. If you cannot accept yourself, if you cannot treat yourself with kindness, you cannot do this for another person.

Very often you behave exactly like your father, but you don't realize it. And though you behave like him, you feel you are total opposites. You do not accept him, you hate him. When you do not accept your father, you do not accept yourself. Your father is in you; you are the continuation of your father. So if you can communicate with yourself, then you can communicate with your father.

The self is made of non-self elements; therefore, understanding ourselves is our practice. Our father is a non-self element. We say our father is not us, but without our father, we cannot exist. So he is fully present in our body and in our mind. He is us. Thus, if you understand yourself, your whole self, you understand that you are your father—he is not outside of you.

There are so many other non-self elements that you can touch and recognize within yourself—your ancestors, the earth, the sun, water, air, all the food you eat, and much more. It may seem like these things are separate from you, but without them, you could not live.

Suppose two warring parties want to negotiate, and both sides do not know enough about themselves. You have to really know yourself, your country, your party, your situation, in order to understand the other's party, the other's nation, the other's people. Self and others are not two separate things, because the suffering, hope, and anger of both sides is very much the same.

When we get angry, we suffer. If you really understand that, you also will be able to understand that when the other person is angry, it means that she is suffering. When someone insults you or behaves violently towards you, you have to be intelligent enough to see that the person suffers from his own violence and anger. But we tend to forget. We think that we are the only one that suffers, and the other person is our oppressor. This is enough to make anger arise, and to strengthen our desire to punish. We want to punish the other person because we suffer. Then, we have anger in us; we have violence in us, just as they do. When we see that our suffering and anger are no different from their suffering and anger, we will behave more compassionately. So understanding the other is understanding yourself, and understanding yourself is understanding the other person. Everything must begin with you.

To understand ourselves, we must learn and practice the way of non-duality. We should not fight our anger, because anger is our self, a part of our self. Anger is of an organic nature, like love. We have to take good care of anger. And because it is an organic entity, an organic phenomenon, it is possible to transform it into another organic entity. The garbage can be transformed back into compost, into lettuce, and into cucumber. So don't despise your anger. Don't fight your anger, and don't suppress your anger. Learn the tender way of taking care of your anger, and transform it into the energy of understanding and compassion.

Compassion Is Intelligent

Understanding and compassion are very powerful sources of energy. They are the opposite of stupidity and passivity. If you think that compassion is passive, weak, or cowardly, then you don't know what real understanding or compassion is. If you think that compassionate people do not resist and challenge injustice, you are wrong. They are warriors, heroes, and heroines who have gained many victories. When you act with compassion, with non-violence, when you act on the basis of non-duality, you have to be very strong. You no longer act out of anger, you do not punish or blame. Compassion grows constantly inside of you, and you can succeed in your fight against injustice. Mahatma Gandhi was just one person. He did not have any bombs, any guns, or any political party. He acted simply on the insight of non-duality, the strength of compassion, not on the basis of anger.

Human beings are not our enemy. Our enemy is not the other person. Our enemy is the violence, ignorance, and injustice in us and in the other person. When we are armed with compassion and understanding, we fight not against other people, but against the tendency to invade, to dominate, and to exploit. We don't want to kill others, but we will not let them dominate and exploit us or other people. You have to protect yourself. You are not stupid. You are very intelligent, and you have insight. Being compassionate does not mean allowing other people to do violence to themselves or to you. Being compassionate means being intelligent. Non-violent action that springs from love can only be intelligent action.

Being compassionate doesn't mean suffering unnecessarily or losing your common sense. Suppose you are leading a group of people doing walking meditation, moving slowly and beautifully. The walking meditation generates a lot of energy; it embraces everyone with calm, solidity, and peace. But suddenly it begins to rain. Would you continue to walk slowly, letting yourself and everyone else get soaked? That's not intelligent. If you are a good leader of the walking meditation, you will break into a jogging meditation. You still maintain the joy of the walking meditation. You can laugh and smile, and thus you prove that the practice is not stupid. You can also be mindful while running and avoid getting soaked. We have to practice in an intelligent way. Meditation is not a stupid act. Meditation is not just blindly following whatever the person next to you does. To meditate you have to be skillful and make good use of your intelligence.

Building a Compassionate Police Force

To be kind does not mean to be passive. To be compassionate does not mean to allow others to walk all over you, to allow yourself to be destroyed. You have to protect yourself and protect others. If you need to lock someone up because he is dangerous, then you have to do that. But you have to do it with compassion. Your motivation is to prevent that person from continuing his course of destruction and from feeding his anger.

You don't have to be a monk in order to be compassionate, you can be a policeman. You can be a judge or a prison guard. But as a policeman, a judge, or prison guard, we need you to be a Bodhisattva. We need you to be beings of great compassion. Although you have to be very firm, you should always keep compassion alive in you.

And if you practice mindful living, you have to help the policeman act out of compassion and non-fear. The police in our time are full of fear, anger, and stress, because they have been assaulted many times. Those who hate the police and insult them don't understand the police yet. In the morning, when the police put on their uniform and guns, they are not sure that they will return home alive in the evening. The police suffer very much. Their families suffer very much. They don't enjoy beating people. They don't enjoy shooting people. But because they do not know how to handle the blocks of fear, suffering, and violence in them, they also can become victims of society like other people. So, as a police chief, if you really understand the minds and hearts of the people on your police force, you will train yourself in such a way that compassion and understanding will be born in your heart. Then you will be able to educate and help the policemen and women who have to go out on the streets every morning, every night, to do the hard task of keeping the city in peace.

In France the police are called "peace-keepers." But if you don't have peace in you, how can you keep peace in the city? You have to keep peace in yourself first. And peace here means non-fear, intelligence, and insight. The police do learn a number of techniques in order to protect themselves, but self-defense techniques are not enough. You have to be intelligent. You have to act out of non-fear. If you are too fearful, then you will make many mistakes. You will be tempted to use your gun, and you may kill many innocent people.

We Cannot Take Sides

In Los Angeles, four policemen beat a black driver nearly to death. The press talked about it all over the world, and everyone wanted to take sides. You may have taken the side of the victim of the beating, or of the policemen. When you judge and take sides, you act as though you are outside of the conflict. You act as though you are not the black driver who was beaten, or the four policemen. But looking deeply, you see that you are the victim of the beating, and you are also the four policemen who did the beating. Anger, fear, frustration, and violence are in the person who was beaten and in those who did the beating. Just as they are in us.

To understand the police and help them suffer less, let us imagine that we are the husband or wife of a police officer. Living together, you are in touch with how hard your spouse's life is. So every morning and every evening, you want to do something to help your spouse to transform his or her anger, fear, and frustration. When you are capable of helping your husband or wife suffer less, then the whole city will profit—even the delinquent youth. This is the best way to help the community. With intelligence, insight, and compassion, you can help avoid a lot of accidents.

A Dialogue to End Anger and Violence

The image of a police officer full of violence, prejudice, and fear is not a positive image. So many young people see the police as their enemy. They want to burn police cars and beat up policemen, because the police are the object of their anger, their frustration. We must organize a meeting, a dialogue, between police and the youngsters who have committed acts of violence, and who have been put in prison. Why don't we organize this kind of conversation and give the police a chance to speak about their frustration, anger, and fear? And why don't we allow these youngsters who fight with the police to speak out about their frustration, anger, and fear? Why don't we televise this dialogue so that a whole nation can learn from it?

This would be true meditation: looking deeply, not as an individual, but as a city, as a nation. We have not seen the truth. We have seen a lot of movies, detective stories, and Westerns, but we have not seen the truth that is in the hearts and minds of real people. We should organize this kind of dialogue so that the truth can be shown to the whole population.

Bombing Ourselves

"God, please forgive them, because they do not know what they are doing," said Christ. When someone commits a crime and makes others suffer, it is because he does not know what he is doing. Many young people commit crimes, and they do not know, they do not understand how much suffering their violence causes. Every time they commit an act of violence, they are doing it to themselves as well as others. They may feel that committing these acts of violence and expressing anger will lessen their anger. But the anger in them will only continue to grow.

When you drop bombs on your enemy, you drop the same bombs on yourself, on your own country. During the war in Vietnam, the American people suffered just as much as the Vietnamese people. The wounds of war are as deep in America as in Vietnam. Stopping violence is what we have to do. And we cannot stop violence unless we have the insight that what we do to the other person, we are doing to ourselves. Teachers must show students that when they are violent, they themselves will suffer. But teachers cannot just tell them this, they have to be more creative than that. We should not be dogmatic in our way of sharing insight with others. We should be flexible and intelligent, using "skillful means." Skillful means is very important. A Great Being has to be skillful in the practice and in helping other people.

Stopping Wars Before They Happen

The majority of us wait until a war breaks out in order to begin some kind of effort to stop it. Many of us do not know that the roots of war are everywhere, including in our own thinking and way of life. We are not capable of seeing the war while it is still hidden. We begin to focus our attention on the war only when the war breaks out into the open and people start talking about it. Then we feel overwhelmed by the intensity of the war. We feel helpless. We take sides and feel that one is right and the other is wrong. We condemn one side, but we have nothing to contribute towards ending the destruction caused by the war.

As a true practitioner, you have to practice looking deeply into the situation to see the war before it starts. You have to begin acting in order to stop the war before it breaks out into the open. With your insight and awareness, you can help other people to wake up and develop the same awareness. Then, together you can act skillfully in order to prevent the war from breaking out into the open.

The countries of NATO thought that violence, bombing Belgrade, was the only solution to ending racial discrimination in the former Yugoslavia. They believed that there was no other way. They were not able to see and respond to the roots of war, which were already apparent before the war started, because their capacity of looking deeply, of meditation is limited. Violence can never bring about peace and understanding. Only by looking deeply in order to understand the true roots of violence can we achieve peace.

If you are a good meditator, you may have deeper insight than others, and you may know better ways to stop racial discrimination without resorting to bombs or other violent means. There are many wars about to break out everywhere on the planet. If you are really a person of peace, you should be aware of that, and try your best, together with your community, to stop these wars before they blow up, causing extreme violence. If you want to stop violent interventions like the one in Kosovo, then you have to offer an alternative. If you have a good idea, you can transmit that idea to your congressperson or senator and urge them to intervene so that a more positive course of action can be taken. We need to learn to meditate as a nation, not only as individuals, in order to achieve the kind of insight that will be able to stop war and violence.

Collective Insight

There is a young man who is a vegetarian, not because he is fanatic or dogmatic, but out of mindfulness. He does not eat the flesh of animals because he doesn't have the heart to eat them. His father was very unhappy about this, and so there was no harmony or joy in his home. The young man knew that he could not stop being vegetarian, because he would be miserable if he had to eat animals. He could not change just to please his father, but he did not want this tense atmosphere to continue. He used his intelligence; he did not remain passive.

One day he came home with a videotape, and said, "Dad, here's a wonderful documentary film." He then showed a video about the slaughter of animals to his father and the whole family. His father experienced so much suffering in watching animals being slaughtered that after having seen that film, he did not want to eat meat anymore. The insight was direct; it was not an idea. Instead of using anger, instead of letting suffering overwhelm him, the young man acted out of loving-kindness, wisdom, and intelligence. He was able to convince the whole family not to eat animals so that compassion could be nourished within each one of them. The act of showing that documentary film was very skillful, and full of love. With skillful action, you can win a very big victory.

As an individual, you may have some insight, and that insight gives rise to compassion and a willingness to act. But as an individual, you can only do so much. If other people do not have the same insight, you have to do your best to make your insight a collective one. Yet you cannot force your insight on others. You may force them to accept your idea, but then it is simply an idea, not a real insight. Insight is not an idea. The way to share your insight is to help create the conditions so that others can realize the same insight—through their own experience, not just believing what you say. This takes skillfulness and patience.

Helping Love to Reappear

There is a sister in Plum Village who is still very young—twenty-two. She was able to help a mother and daughter to reconcile just after they vowed never to see each other again. In a period of three hours, she was able to help the mother and the daughter resolve their conflict. In the end, both of them practiced hugging meditation. They gently took each other in their arms and breathed in and out mindfully several times. They practiced, "Breathing in, I am aware that I am alive; breathing out, I am aware that my beloved one is still alive, here in my arms." They practiced to be mindful of the gift of each other's presence and were deeply in touch with the present moment, putting one hundred percent of themselves in the act of embracing the other. It was very healing. Through the practice, they realized that they loved each other very much. They did not know that they loved each other so much, because they had not been skillful in their relationship, in their way of speaking and listening.

Just because anger or hate is present does not mean that

the capacity to love and accept is not there. If you are skillful as a meditator, as a peace-worker, you can help the love, the understanding to reappear in yourself and the other person. Please do not believe that love is not in you. It's not true; love is always in you. It is like the sunshine; even when it rains, the sunshine is always there a little bit above the clouds. If you go above the clouds, you see plenty of sunshine. So if you believe that there is no love in you, that you feel only hate for the other person, you are wrong. Wait until the other person dies. You will cry and cry and wish that he could come back to life. This shows that love is there. You should give love a chance to manifest, while the other person is still alive. To help love to reappear you have to know how to manage your anger. Anger always goes together with confusion, with ignorance.

Going Past Judgment

Suppose you are the teacher of a five-year-old girl. When her mother comes to pick her up from school, you see that the mother is aggressive, making the little girl suffer. What can you do? You can do a lot. The child will listen to you, so you can help her to understand her mother. You can also give her a chance to speak out and tell you of the difficulties she has with her mother, even though she is only five. You can play the role of a good mother for her. You can tell her that it is possible for the two of you to help her mother. You can teach her how to act and react in moments when the mother becomes angry and violent to avoid making the situation worse. It is very important to help the little girl, because when there is a change in her, it will have a good effect on the mother.

As the teacher of the young girl, you also have access to the mother. If you have compassion and insight you will be able to help. Otherwise, you will only judge the mother as wrong and the daughter as right. You will only be able to condemn the mother's abusive behavior. You oppose her violence with her child, but it is not helpful just to express your disapproval. You have to do something. You have to act out of compassion and insight, not only for the abused child, but also for the child's mother and father. If you cannot help her father and mother, you cannot help the child. You may see the child as the victim, as the only one who needs help. But if you really want to do everything you can to help the child, you must help the mother and father—who you considered to be the enemy. If you do not help them you cannot help the child. Helping the parents is helping the child. The parents are full of ignorance, they are full of violence and anger, and that is why their child suffers. So you have to have compas-

sion towards the parents. You have to see the roots of the suffering. Our educators need to know this and help all of us
take care of parents in order to take care of children.

Serving Our Country

The French government is trying hard to take care of youngsters who are violent. They do have some insight. They understand that the violence and the suffering of these
youngsters are caused by society. In order to know how to respond, we must listen like a doctor. We must listen very carefully to the organism of society, to see why the youngsters
become so violent, so angry. If we do this, we will see that the
roots of their anger and violence are in the family, in the way
parents conduct their daily life. And the roots of family violence are found in the way society is organized and how people consume.

The government is also people. The government is made
of fathers, of mothers, of sons, of daughters. And these fathers, mothers, sons, and daughters also carry the violence of
their family within them. So if the French prime minister
does not practice looking deeply, does not see the anger, violence, depression, and suffering within himself, he will not

be able to understand the violence, anger, and depression in the younger generation. He also has to understand members of his government, in the ministry of youth, in the ministry of education, etc., and see their suffering. As citizens, as a government, we must act, but on what basis should that action take place? On the basis of understanding.

If we have practiced looking deeply enough in order to see the roots of anger and violence in our society, then we will have a lot of compassion for our young people. We will know that just locking them up and punishing them is not going to help. This is what the former French Prime Minister Jospin has said. So he and his government do have some insight. But as a people, as citizens, we have to help. We have to help deepen this kind of insight. As an educator, as a parent, as an artist, as a writer, we have to practice so that we have enough insight to help our government.

Even if you are in a different political party than the ruling party, you have to practice. When you help the ruling party, you are helping your country. It is your country that you must help, not a political party. And if the current French prime minister now has a chance to do something to improve the condition of the young people in France, then the appropriate way to serve your country is to offer him your insight and your help. This does not mean you betray your people or your party. Your party exists in order to serve your country, not to create difficulties for another party or the party in power. So, as a politician, you have to practice nonduality. You have to see that compassion is above any political affiliation. This is not partisan politics but intelligent politics. They are politics that are humane, that aim at the well-being and the transformation of society, not just at gaining power.

EIGHT

DAVID AND ANGELINA: THE HABIT ENERGY OF ANGER

There was a young man named David. He was a very handsome young man and quite intelligent. He was born into a rich family and had everything he needed to be successful. But he did not enjoy life. He was not capable of being happy. He had a lot of problems with his parents, brothers, and sisters. He did not know how to communicate. He was a very egotistical person, so he always blamed his father, his mother, his sister, and his brothers for his misery. He suffered a lot, but he was not miserable because everyone hated him, or because everyone wanted to punish him. He was miserable because he was not capable of loving, of understanding. He was able to make friends for a few days, but soon after that his friends would leave him because it was quite difficult to be around him. He was very arrogant, very self-centered, and he lacked understanding and compassion.

One day he went to a Buddhist temple in the town, but not to listen to a dharma talk. He did not care about dharma talks. He went with the hope of making new friends because he was in desperate need of a friend. So far no one had been able to remain his friend. He was rich, he was handsome, and many people were interested in getting to know him. But all of them abandoned him after a short time.

So that morning he went to the temple because life without a friend was hell. He was thirsty for a friend, for a partner, even if he was not capable of keeping a friend or a partner. And when he came to the temple, he passed a group of people coming out, and among them was a very beautiful young lady. The image of the young lady moved him deeply, and he was love-struck, dumbfounded. He was no longer interested in entering the temple anymore, and he turned around in order to follow the group. Unfortunately, another group of people came streaming in, and the crowd made it difficult for David to leave. When he managed to get out of the temple, the group and the beautiful lady had vanished.

He searched all over for one hour but could not find her, and he went home carrying that beautiful image in his heart. He could not sleep that night, or the next night. And then on the third night, he saw a beautiful old man with a white beard in his dream. The old man said, "If you want to meet her, then go to the Eastern market today." Though it wasn't morning yet, he did not feel like sleeping anymore. He got up and waited until noon before setting out on his search for the young lady.

When he arrived at the Eastern market, there were not many people. It was still too early, so he went into a bookshop and began to look around. Suddenly, he looked up and he saw a painting of a very beautiful young lady hanging on the wall. It was the same young lady he had seen three days before at the temple. The same eyes, the same nose, the same mouth. In the dream, he was told he would meet that lady in the market, but maybe this was what the old man meant—the picture was all he could have. "Maybe I deserve only an image," he thought. "I don't deserve a reality." So instead of buying books, he used all his money to buy that painting. He brought it home, and he hung it on the wall of his dormitory room at college.

He was a lonely person. He did not have friends. Often he did not go to the campus cafeteria. Instead, he stayed home and ate instant noodles. You may have already guessed that David is Asian. That day, he prepared two bowls of instant noodles, and two pairs of chopsticks. The second bowl was for the lady in the painting. He enjoyed his noodles, and from time to time he looked up and invited the lady in the painting to eat.

We know that there are people who cannot communicate with human beings. They have a cat or a dog to live with for company, so that they can pour out all their love and care on it. They buy the most expensive food for their pet. For many people, it is much easier to love a cat or a dog because they never argue with you. When you say something that is not nice, they don't react. The same thing was true with David. He could live in peace with the lady in the painting, but if the real lady were there, he might not be able to live with her for more than twenty-four hours.

One day he could not finish his bowl of noodles. Life seemed to have no flavor at all. He had had it up to his neck. At that moment, he looked up at the painting. He was about to ask, "What's the use of living anyway?" when he saw the lady blink her eyes and smile. He was very startled. He thought that he was in a dream. He rubbed his eyes and looked up again, and there she was, perfectly still. A few days later, he saw the lady smile and blink her eyes again. He was very surprised. He continued to look at her, and suddenly she became a real person and stepped down from the painting. Her name was Angelina, because she came from heaven. You cannot imagine how happy the young man was. He was in paradise. To have such a beautiful young lady as a friend, what could be more wonderful?

But you may have already guessed the rest of the story. He

was not capable of being happy even with someone as fresh and kind as Angelina. And three or four months later, she left him. It was impossible to live with someone like David. One morning he woke up and found a note on his desk. The young lady had gone for good. She wrote: "David, it is impossible to live with you. You are too self-centered, you have no capacity to listen to anyone. You are intelligent, handsome, and rich. But you don't know how to maintain a relationship with another human being." That morning, David wanted to kill himself. He thought that if he could not even manage to live with such a sweet, beautiful lady, then he must be worthless. He looked for a piece of rope to hang himself with.

Every year in France, twelve thousand people commit suicide. That is about thirty-three every day. That's far too many. And David is among them, waiting for you to rescue him. In the United States and throughout Europe, the rate of suicide is very much the same. People are overwhelmed by despair. For many of us, communication has become impossible and life no longer has meaning.

Offering the Incense of the Heart

While David was tying a knot in the rope, he suddenly remembered that one day Angelina smiled and said, "David, if someday I'm no longer around and you miss me very much, just burn some incense." The day she said this, she had been able to convince him to come to the temple with her to listen to a dharma talk. There, the monk was explaining how to offer incense as a way of communicating. When you burn incense, you want to communicate with the Buddha, with the Bodhisattvas, with our ancestors. If we can communicate with our ancestors, we can communicate also with our brothers and sisters around us. So the monk was talking about communicating through the act of offering incense. He said that the incense we offer should be the incense of our heart: the incense of mindfulness, the incense of concentration, the incense of wisdom, of insight. David was there sitting close to Angelina, but he did not listen very deeply. However, he heard enough to remember that event. After both of them left the temple, Angelina turned to him and said, "David, if someday you want to get in touch with me, offer some incense."

Remembering this, he dropped the rope, ran to the store nearby and bought a bundle of incense. But David did not know how to burn incense. In Plum Village every time we offer incense, we use only one stick. He used the whole bundle, and in just a few minutes, his room was filled with smoke. He waited for fifteen minutes, half an hour, one hour, but Angelina did not show up. So then he remembered what the monk said—"For true communication to be possible, you have to offer the incense of the heart, namely the incense of mindfulness. The incense of concentration, the incense of insight." Burning incense without mindfulness wouldn't work.

David sat there and thought deeply about his situation. He saw that he had not succeeded with his parents, with his brothers and sisters, with his friends, with his society. He had even failed with Angelina. He began to see that he always blamed other people for his suffering. This was the first time he had a few moments of concentration and he began to have some insight. This was the first time in his life he sat down quietly and saw that he had been unjust to his parents, and that communication was not possible partly because of him. He had blamed everyone. He hadn't understood until now that he was responsible. Even with such a sweet and beautiful person like Angelina, he had not succeeded.

For the first time, tears ran down his cheeks, and he was truly sorry for the way he had treated his parents, brothers, sisters, and friends. He remembered the time he came home drunk, very late at night, beat Angelina and abused her. He thought of all of this, and suddenly a drop of compassion penetrated his heart, a heart so full of suffering and afflictions. And he continued crying. The more he cried, the more refreshed he felt in his heart. A transformation took place within him. He began to understand what Angelina had tried to tell him, about how to live according to the Five Mindfulness Trainings, about practicing deep listening and loving speech. He felt a willingness to begin anew, and he told himself that if Angelina ever came back, he would be a different person. "I will know how to take care of her, and how to make happiness possible." At that moment there was a knock on the door. Angelina was back. Although David had practiced barely one hour, his transformation was profound.

David and Angelina Are Among Us

Do not think that David is only a person in a story, a person of the past. No. David is still alive; he sits here among us. Angelina, too. Remember that David was intelligent, handsome, but he had a very strong habit energy of always blaming others for his misery. He couldn't communicate with his parents, his brothers, his sisters, or his friends. He made them suffer. He did not want to make them unhappy, but his habit energy was too strong, so he could not avoid it. He was lonely, and he thought that he was the only one in the world who was that lonely. He was thirsty for the understanding of another human being, a person who could stand by his side. All of us have this need—it is very human. We need someone who can really understand us and help us confront the difficulties of life.

So, it is not difficult to understand David. You understand his deepest desire. You understand his difficulties. One day, Angelina stepped into his life. From time to time, this kind of good fortune happens to us, too. Sometimes a very nice person steps into our life. And if we know how to take care of that person, our life becomes more meaningful. But if we don't know how to take care of ourselves and our habit energy, we will not know how to take care of our Angelina. So we become angry with her, and we mistreat her. That is why Angelina has left us, because she suffered so much from our behavior.

Keeping Angelina in Our Life

The minute Angelina stepped down from the painting and became a real person, she smiled a heavenly smile at David. She looked at the bowl of the noodles and she said, "How can you eat such junk food? Just a minute." Then she disappeared. And in no time at all, she reappeared with a basket of green vegetables. She prepared a very delicious bowl of noodles for David quite different from the instant ones he was used to eating.

Angelina is talented. She knows how to make you happy. But you were not grateful, and you lacked understanding.

You were not capable of keeping your Angelina, and that is why she left. Maybe you are Angelina, and because your David was so difficult to be with, you have left your David. Although you did your best to help him, it was impossible to live with him. He was not capable of recognizing that you are his Angelina. His habit energy pushed him to continue to live and consume in a way that poisoned his body and mind. Maybe he went to the bar every night and got drunk. And no matter how much you pleaded with him, he could not stop drinking. And every night he came home drunk and beat you. He was not able to listen to you at all. No matter how hard you tried to be sweet, to be patient, he always cut you off, and didn't allow you to finish your sentence. He was never capable of listening to you. You were patient, but you have your limits. Communication was impossible and so you gave up.

Where Is Your Angelina Now?

Who is David, and who is Angelina? I would like you to answer this question. Are you David? If you are David, then where is your Angelina now? Is she still with you, or has she left you? What have you done to her? How did you treat her?

Did you take good care of her? Were you able to make her happy? We have to ask ourselves all these questions. "Where is my Angelina now? Where is she? What have I done to her?" These are very important questions that help us to look deeply.

This is a meditation, true meditation. David might be your partner. Angelina might be your partner. Angelina can be a man or a woman, David as well. Angelina stepped into your life. In the beginning you were so happy to be with her, you cherished her presence. You thought that with her, life was possible again. But you were not able to maintain that kind of awareness. You lost the awareness that Angelina was life's gift to you. You made her suffer so much that she left you. There was a time when she pleaded with you to practice the Five Mindfulness Trainings, but because of your strong habit energy, you never accepted. She begged you to consume in moderation, and to stop smoking and drinking. She invited you to use loving speech, to listen deeply, to associate with good people and not with those who water negative seeds in you. But you never listened to her. You continued with your way of life, pushed by your habit energy, and that is why she had to leave.

Your Angelina may be your daughter or your son. He or she has come into your life. How have you treated him or her?

Are you able to live with your son or your daughter in harmony, peace, and love? Or are you having difficulties with your Angelina? Maybe your Angelina has left home. In the story, David was about to commit suicide after the departure of Angelina. But he remembered the talk he heard about the practice of communicating through incense, and suddenly his despair turned into hope. He believed that if he offered the incense of mindfulness and concentration, Angelina would come back to him. He had an opportunity to sit down, to think, and to look back into his life.

Beginning Anew

In our daily life we run continuously. We do not have the capacity or the opportunity to stop and look deeply into our life. We must look back, and look deeply in order to understand. David sat for forty-five minutes in his room, looking back at his life. He gained a lot of insight and he began to cry. He cried for the first time in his life because he recognized his habit energy and the damage he had caused to the people around him, his parents, his friends, his brothers and sisters, and himself.

We may practice sitting meditation everyday, but have we

had this kind of insight? In your sitting meditation, you have to see your Angelina stepping into your life as an angel. You have to see how things have deteriorated between you and her: how you treated her, how you made her suffer, and how she left you. When you can look into your relationship in this way, you are practicing deep meditation. The insight you get will tell you exactly what to do and what not to do. It is possible for you to offer the incense of the heart and call your Angelina back. Angelina is always there. Love is still in her heart. She is ready to forgive, if you know how to burn the incense of your heart, the incense of the Mindfulness Trainings, concentration, and insight.

You may be a lucky person, because more than one Angelina has stepped into your life. Your partner, your son, your daughter, your father, your mother are also your Angelinas. The practice is to call your Angelina by his or her true name, to recognize and appreciate that he or she is your Angelina. Do not say that no Angelina has ever come into your life. That's not true. Sit mindfully and silently call her name, his name. "My Angelina, I'm sorry. You have stepped into my life, and I have made you suffer. I have made myself suffer at the same time. I did not mean to. I was unskillful. I did not know how to protect myself, and protect you, with the practice of the Mindfulness Trainings. I want to begin anew." If you really practice like this, Angelina will come back to you.

Protecting My Angelinas

I am a David also. I have many Angelinas in my life. And in my small meditation hall, I have a picture of about one hundred of my Angelinas—they are my students who live in our practice centers in France and the United States. Before I practice sitting meditation, I always look at that picture and bow to all my Angelinas. Then I sit down and I vow to live in such a way that my Angelinas will never leave me. I vow to practice mindful speech, to practice the Mindfulness Trainings, and not to betray my Angelinas. By doing so, I avoid causing suffering to my Angelinas and I am able bring them joy. This makes me very happy.

If your Angelina has left you, what will you do to bring her back into your life? Your Angelina still may be with you, but about to leave you, or your Angelina may have already left you. In both cases the practice of protection is relevant, because the practice can help you to keep her or to bring her back to you. Please do not get lost in abstract notions. Spiritual teachings are alive, and they can help you to protect your Angelina. True wisdom and compassion are born from touching real suffering. This is the kind of dharma that is appropriate and effective and relevant to the situation. Use all your time and energy to look back and ask yourself these questions: Where is my Angelina now? How have I treated her? And if she has left: What should I do in order to bring her home again?

NINE

———◆◆◆◆———

EMBRACING ANGER
WITH MINDFULNESS

The Knots of Anger

In our consciousness there are blocks of pain, anger, and frustration called internal formations. They are also called knots because they tie us up and obstruct our freedom.

When someone insults us, or does something unkind to us, an internal formation is created in our consciousness. If you don't know how to undo the internal knot and transform it, the knot will stay there for a long time. And the next time someone says something or does something to you of the same nature, that internal formation will grow stronger. As knots or blocks of pain in us, our internal formations have the power to push us, to dictate our behavior.

After a while, it becomes very difficult for us to transform, to undo the knots, and we cannot ease the constriction of this crystallized formation. The Sanskrit word for internal formation is *samyojana*. It means "to crystallize." Every one of us has internal formations that we need to take care of. With the practice of meditation we can undo these knots and experience transformation and healing.

Not all internal formations are unpleasant. There are also pleasant internal formations, but they can still make us suffer. When you taste, hear, or see something pleasant, then that pleasure can become a strong internal knot. When the object of your pleasure disappears, you miss it and you begin searching for it. You spend a lot of time and energy trying to experience it again. If you smoke marijuana or drink alcohol, and begin to like it, then it becomes an internal formation in your body and in your mind. You cannot get it off your mind. You will always look for more. The strength of the internal knot is pushing you and controlling you. So internal formations deprive us of our freedom.

Falling in love is a big internal formation. Once you are in love, you think only of the other person. You are not free anymore. You cannot do anything; you cannot study, you cannot work, you cannot enjoy the sunshine or the beauty of nature around you. You can think only of the object of your love. That is why we speak about it as a kind of accident, "falling in love." You fall down. You are not stable anymore because you have gotten into an accident. So love can also be an internal knot.

Pleasant or unpleasant, both kinds of knots take away our liberty. That is why we should guard our body and our mind very carefully, to prevent these knots from taking root in us. Drugs, alcohol, and tobacco can create internal formations in our body. And anger, craving, jealousy, despair can create internal formations in our mind.

Training in Aggression

Anger is an internal formation, and since it makes us suffer, we try our best to get rid of it. Psychologists like the expression "getting it out of your system." And they speak about venting anger, like ventilating a room filled with smoke. Some psychologists say that when the energy of anger arises in you, you should ventilate it by hitting a pillow, kicking something, or by going into the forest to yell and shout.

As a kid you were not supposed to say certain swear words. Your parents may not have allowed you to say these words, because they are harmful, they damage relationships.

So you went into the woods or to an isolated place and shouted these words very clearly, very strongly, in order to relieve the feeling of oppression. This is also venting.

People who use venting techniques like hitting a pillow or shouting are actually rehearsing anger. When someone is angry and vents their anger by hitting a pillow, they are learning a dangerous habit. They are training in aggression. Instead, we generate the energy of mindfulness and embrace anger every time it manifests.

Treating Anger with Tenderness

Mindfulness does not fight anger or despair. Mindfulness is there in order to recognize. To be mindful of something is to recognize that something is there in the present moment. Mindfulness is the capacity of being aware of what is going on in the present moment. "Breathing in I know that anger has manifested in me; breathing out I smile towards my anger." This is not an act of suppression or of fighting. It is an act of recognizing. Once we recognize our anger, we embrace it with a lot of awareness, a lot of tenderness.

When it is cold in your room, you turn on the heater, and the heater begins to send out waves of hot air. The cold air doesn't have to leave the room for the room to become warm.

The cold air is embraced by the hot air and becomes warm—there's no fighting at all between them.

We practice taking care of our anger in the same way. Mindfulness recognizes anger, is aware of its presence, accepts and allows it to be there. Mindfulness is like a big brother who does not suppress his younger brother's suffering. He simply says, "Dear brother, I'm here for you." You take your younger brother in your arms and you comfort him. This is exactly our practice.

Imagine a mother getting angry with her baby and hitting him when he cries. That mother does not know that she and her baby are one. We are mothers of our anger, and we have to help our baby, our anger, not fight and destroy it. Our anger is us, and our compassion is also us. To meditate does not mean to fight. In Buddhism, the practice of meditation should be the practice of embracing and transforming, not of fighting.

Using Anger, Using Suffering

To grow the tree of enlightenment, we must make good use of our afflictions, our suffering. It is like growing lotus flowers; we cannot grow a lotus on marble. We cannot grow a lotus without mud.

Practitioners of meditation do not discriminate against or reject their internal formations. We do not transform ourselves into a battlefield, good fighting evil. We treat our afflictions, our anger, our jealousy with a lot of tenderness. When anger comes up in us, we should begin to practice mindful breathing right away: "Breathing in, I know that anger is in me. Breathing out, I am taking good care of my anger." We behave exactly like a mother: "Breathing in, I know that my child is crying. Breathing out, I will take good care of my child." This is the practice of compassion.

If you don't know how to treat yourself with compassion, how can you treat another person with compassion? When anger arises, continue to practice mindful breathing and mindful walking to generate the energy of mindfulness. Continue to tenderly embrace the energy of anger within you. Anger may continue to be there for some time, but you are safe, because the Buddha is in you, helping you to take good care of your anger. The energy of mindfulness is the energy of the Buddha. When you practice mindful breathing and embracing your anger, you are under the protection of the Buddha. There is no doubt about it: the Buddha is embracing you and your anger with a lot of compassion.

Giving and Receiving
Mindfulness Energy

When you are angry, when you feel despair, you practice mindful breathing and mindful walking, to generate the energy of mindfulness. This energy allows you to recognize and embrace your painful feelings. And if your mindfulness is not strong enough, you ask a brother or a sister in the practice to sit close to you, to breathe with you, to walk with you in order to support you with his or her mindfulness energy.

Practicing mindfulness does not mean that you have to do everything on your own. You can practice with the support of your friends. They can generate enough mindfulness energy to help you take care of your strong emotions.

We can also support others with our mindfulness when they are in difficulty. When our child is drowning in a strong emotion, we can hold his or her hand and say, "My dear one, breathe. Breathe in and out with Mommy, with Daddy." We can also invite our child to do walking meditation with us, gently taking her hand and helping her calm down, with each step. When you give your child some of your mindfulness energy, she will be able to calm down very quickly and embrace her emotions.

Recognizing, Embracing, Relieving the Suffering of Anger

The first function of mindfulness is to recognize, not to fight. "Breathing in, I know that anger has manifested in me. Hello, my little anger." And breathing out, "I will take good care of you."

Once we have recognized our anger, we embrace it. This is the second function of mindfulness, and it is a very pleasant practice. Instead of fighting, we are taking good care of our emotion. If you know how to embrace your anger, something will change.

We have said many times that it is like cooking potatoes. You cover the pot and then the water will begin to boil. You must keep the stove on for at least twenty minutes for the potatoes to cook. Your anger is a kind of potato and you cannot eat a raw potato.

Mindfulness is like the fire cooking the potatoes of anger. The first few minutes of recognizing and embracing your anger with tenderness can bring results. You get some relief. Anger is still there, but you do not suffer so much anymore, because you know how to take care of your baby. So the third function of mindfulness is soothing, relieving. Anger is there, but it is being taken care of. The situation is no longer in chaos, with the crying baby left all alone. The mother is there to take care of the baby and the situation is under control.

Keeping Mindfulness Alive

And who is this mother? The mother is the living Buddha. The capacity of being mindful, the capacity of being understanding, loving, and caring is the Buddha in us. Every time we are capable of generating mindfulness, it makes the Buddha in us a reality. With the Buddha in you, you have nothing to worry about anymore. Everything will be fine if you know how to keep the Buddha within you alive.

It is important to recognize that we always have the Buddha in us. Even if we are angry, unkind, or in despair, the Buddha is always within us. This means we always have the potential to be mindful, to be understanding, to be loving.

We need to practice mindful breathing or walking in order to touch the Buddha within us. When you touch the seed of mindfulness that lies in your consciousness, the Buddha will manifest in your mind consciousness and embrace your anger. You don't have to worry, just continue to practice breathing or walking to keep the Buddha alive. Then everything will be fine. The Buddha recognizes. The Buddha embraces. The Buddha relieves, and the Buddha looks deeply into the nature of anger. The Buddha understands. And this understanding will bring about transformation.

The energy of mindfulness contains the energy of concentration as well as the energy of insight. Concentration helps you to focus on just one thing. With concentration, the energy of looking becomes more powerful. Because of that, it can make a breakthrough that is insight. Insight always has the power of liberating you. If mindfulness is there, and you know how to keep mindfulness alive, concentration will be there, too. And if you know how to keep concentration alive, insight will also come. So mindfulness recognizes, embraces, and relieves. Mindfulness helps us look deeply in order to gain insight. Insight is the liberating factor. It is what frees us and allows transformation to happen. This is the Buddhist practice of taking care of anger.

The Basement and the Living Room

Let us use a house to represent our consciousness. We can identify two parts: the basement is the store consciousness and the living area is mind consciousness. Internal formations, like anger, rest in the store consciousness—in the basement—in the form of a seed, until you hear, see, read, or think of something that touches your seed of anger. Then it comes up and manifests on the level of your mind consciousness, your living room. It manifests as a zone of energy that makes the atmosphere in your living room heavy and unpleasant. When the energy of anger comes up, we suffer.

Whenever anger manifests, the practitioner immediately invites the energy of mindfulness to manifest also, through the practice of mindful walking and mindful breathing. This way, another zone of energy—the energy of mindfulness—is created. It is so important to learn how to practice walking and breathing mindfully, how to practice cleaning and working mindfully, how to practice mindfulness in our daily life. Then, every time a negative energy manifests, we will know how to generate the energy of mindfulness in order to embrace it and take care of it.

The Mind Needs Good Circulation, Too

There are toxins in our body and, if our blood does not circulate well, these toxins will accumulate in certain places. In order to remain healthy, our organism has to expel these toxins. Massaging will stimulate the blood circulation. When the blood circulates well, it can nourish organs like the kidneys, the liver, and the lungs so that they can expel toxins from the body. Therefore it is important to have good blood circulation. Drinking a lot of water and practicing deep breathing can also help expel toxins from the body, through the skin, lungs, urine, and excrement. All practices that help eliminate toxins from our system are very important.

Now suppose I have a very painful spot in my body, because a lot of toxins have accumulated there. Every time I touch this spot, it hurts; this is equivalent to touching an internal knot in the mind. The energy of mindfulness, the practice of mindfulness, is like the practice of massaging an internal formation. You may have a block of suffering, pain, sorrow, or despair in you and this is a poison, a toxin in your consciousness. You have to practice mindfulness in order to embrace and transform the toxin.

Embracing your pain and sorrow with the energy of mindfulness is exactly the practice of massaging, not our body, but our consciousness. Our consciousness may be in a situation of bad circulation. When the blood does not circulate well, then our organs cannot function properly and we get sick. When our psyche does not circulate well, then our mind will become sick. Mindfulness is an energy that stimulates and accelerates circulation throughout blocks of pain.

Occupying the Living Room

Our blocks of pain, sorrow, anger, and despair always want to come up into our mind consciousness, into our living room, because they have grown big and need our attention. They want to emerge, but we don't want them to come up because they are painful to look at. So we try to block their way. We want them to stay asleep down in the basement. Because we do not want to face them, our habit is to fill our living room with other guests. But whenever we have ten or fifteen minutes of free time, and we don't know what to do, these internal knots will come up and make a mess in the living room. To avoid this, we pick up a book, we turn on the television, we go for a drive, we do anything to keep our living room occupied. When the living room is occupied, these unpleasant internal formations will not come up.

All mental formations need to circulate, but we don't want them to come up because we don't want to feel the pain. We want them to stay locked away. We are very afraid, because we believe that if we allow them to come up, we will suffer a lot. That is why our daily habit is to fill up the living room with guests, like television, books, magazines, and conversations, in order to keep these internal formations from surfacing. When we continue to do this, we create bad circulation in our psyche, and symptoms of mental illness and depression begin to appear. They may manifest in our body or in our mind.

Sometimes when we have a headache, we take aspirin, but our headache does not go away. This kind of headache can be a symptom of mental illness. Sometimes we have allergies. We think that it is a physical problem, but allergies can also be a symptom of mental illness. We are advised by doctors to take drugs, and so we continue to suppress our internal formations, making our sickness worse.

Making Your Unwanted Guests Feel at Home

When you remove the embargo and the blocks of pain come up, you will have to suffer a bit. There is no way to avoid it. And that is why the Buddha said that you have to learn how to embrace this pain. It is for this reason that the practice of mindfulness is so important. You generate a strong source of energy so that you can recognize, embrace, and take care of these negative energies. And since the Buddha is in you as the energy of mindfulness, you invite Buddha to come up and help you embrace the internal knots. If they don't want to come up, you coax them to come up. After being embraced for some time, they will return back to the basement and become seeds again.

For instance, the Buddha said that all of us have the seed of fear, but most of us suppress it and keep it locked in the dark. To help us identify, embrace, and look deeply at the seeds of fear, he offered us the practice of the Five Remembrances:

- *I am of the nature to grow old. I cannot escape old age.*
- *I am of the nature to have ill health. I cannot escape ill health.*
- *I am of the nature to die. I cannot escape dying.*
- *All that is dear to me and everyone I love are of the nature to change. There is no way to escape being separated from them. I cannot keep anything. I come here empty-handed, and I go empty-handed.*
- *My actions are my only true belongings. I cannot escape the consequences of my actions. My actions are the ground on which I stand.*

Every day we have to practice like this, taking a few moments to contemplate each exercise as we follow our breathing. We practice the Five Remembrances so that the seed of fear can circulate. We must invite it up to be recognized, to be embraced. And then when it goes back down again, it becomes smaller.

When we invite our seed of fear up like this, we will be better equipped to take care of our anger. Fear gives life to anger. You don't have peace when fear is there, so it becomes the soil on which anger can grow. Fear is based on ignorance, and this lack of understanding is also a primary cause of anger.

Every time you give your internal formations a bath of mindfulness, the blocks of pain in you become lighter and less dangerous. So give your anger, your despair, your fear a bath of mindfulness every day—that is your practice. If mindfulness is not there, it is very unpleasant to have these seeds come up. But if you know how to generate the energy of mindfulness, it is very healing to invite them up every day and embrace them. And after several days or weeks of bringing them up daily and helping them go back down again, you create good circulation in your psyche, and the symptoms of mental illness will begin to disappear.

Mindfulness does the work of massaging your internal formations, your blocks of suffering. You have to allow them to circulate, and this is possible only if you are not afraid of them. If you learn not to fear your knots of suffering, you can learn how to embrace them with the energy of mindfulness and to transform them.

TEN

MINDFUL BREATHING

Breathe to Take Care of Your Anger

When the energy of anger, jealousy, or despair manifests in us, we should know how to handle it, otherwise we will be overwhelmed by it and suffer tremendously. Mindful breathing is the practice that can help us take care of our emotions.

First, in order to take good care of our emotions, we have to learn how to take good care of our body. By becoming aware of breathing in and out we become aware of our body. "Breathing in, I am aware of my whole body, breathing out, I am aware of my whole body." Go back to your body. Embrace it with the energy of mindfulness generated by the practice of mindful breathing.

In daily life, we may be very busy taking care of many things, and we forget how important our body is to us. Our body may be suffering or sick. So we should know how to go back to our body, in order to embrace it tenderly, with mindfulness. As a mother holds her baby tenderly in her arms, we are doing very much the same thing. We go back to our body and we embrace our body with tenderness, with the energy of mindfulness. After having embraced our body as a whole, we begin to embrace all the different parts of our body one by one—our eyes, our nose, our lungs, our heart, our stomach, our kidneys, and so on.

Deep Relaxation for Embracing and Healing Anger

The best position for practicing this is lying down. You focus your attention on a part of your body, such as your heart. As you breathe in, you become aware of your heart, and as you breathe out, you smile towards it. You send it your love, your tenderness.

The energy of mindfulness is like a beam of light that can show us very clearly every part of our body. Modern hospitals have scanners that can scan our body to see each area clearly. But the light beam of the scanner is an X-ray beam, and not the loving beam of mindfulness.

We call this practice of scanning our body with a beam of mindfulness, Deep Relaxation (see text for Deep Relaxation in Appendix D). Another instruction for mindful breathing is "Breathing in, I calm my whole body, breathing out, I calm my whole body." Your body may be agitated and tense, and embracing with the energy of mindfulness can help it to relax and become peaceful again. When the body functions peacefully, it can begin to heal. This helps the mind to relax and also heal.

According to this teaching, our breath is a part of our body. When we are afraid of something or when we are angry, our breath is shallow and the quality of our breathing is very low. Our breath is short, noisy, and not peaceful at all. But if you know how to begin breathing in and breathing out mindfully, calming your breath, then, in just a few minutes, your breath will improve. Your breathing will become lighter, more silent, and more harmonious. And your mind will begin to calm.

Breathing, like meditation, is no less than an art. You have to be very artful handling your in-breath and out-breath, so that harmony can be reestablished in your body and your mind. If you dominate your breath with violence, you cannot create harmony and peace in your body or in your consciousness. Once your breathing has become calmer and deeper, you can continue breathing like this in order to embrace different parts of your body.

While lying down, practice mindful breathing and generate the energy of mindfulness. Scan your body with the loving beam of mindfulness from the top of your head until you arrive at the soles of your feet. It may take half an hour. This is the best way of showing your concern, your love, your attention to your body.

Each of us should be able to do this at least once a day. You can arrange your schedule so that every day, maybe before going to sleep, the whole family can lie down comfortably on the floor and practice total relaxation for twenty or thirty minutes. Turn off the television and invite everyone to come and participate. In the beginning you might like to use a tape to guide the whole family in practicing total relaxation. Later, one of you can lead the practice, helping everyone calm and care for their bodies.

You Can Make It Through the Storm

There are several simple methods for taking care of our strong emotions. One is "belly breathing," breathing from the abdomen. When we are caught in a strong emotion like fear or anger, our practice is to bring our attention down to the abdomen. To stay on the level of the intellect is dangerous. Strong emotions are like a storm, and to stand in the middle of a storm is very dangerous. Yet that is what most of us do when we stay in our minds, letting our feelings overwhelm us. Instead, we have to get rooted by bringing our attention downward. We focus on our abdomen and practice mindful breathing, just giving all of our attention to its rise and fall. We can do this either sitting or lying down.

When you look at a tree in a storm, you see that the top of the tree is very unstable and vulnerable. The wind can break the smaller branches at any time. But when you look down to the trunk of the tree, you have a different impression. You see that the tree is very solid and still, and you know that it will be able to withstand the storm. We are also like a tree. Our head is like the top of the tree during a tempest of a strong emotion, so we have to bring our attention down to the level of our navel. We begin to practice mindful breathing. We concentrate just on our breathing and on the rise and fall of our abdomen. It is a very important practice because it helps us to see that, although an emotion may be very strong, it will stay only for a while and then go; it cannot last forever. If you train yourself to practice like this during difficult times, you will survive these storms.

You have to be aware that your emotion is just an emotion. It comes, stays for some time, and then goes away. Why should someone die because of an emotion? You are more than your emotions. It is important to remember this. During a crisis, when you breathe in and out, maintain the awareness that your emotion will go away if you continue to practice. After you have succeeded a few times, you will have confidence in yourself and in the practice. Let us not get caught by our thoughts and feelings. Let us bring our attention down to our belly and breathe in and out. This storm will go away, so don't be afraid.

Recognizing and Embracing Mental Formations

We embrace our bodies with mindfulness in order to calm them. We can do the same with mental formations: "Breathing in, I am aware of my mental formations. Breathing out, I am aware of my mental formations." In Buddhist psychology there are fifty-one mental formations. There are negative mental formations, like anger, craving, and jealousy, and there are positive mental formations, like mindfulness and equanimity.

When we experience a positive mental formation like joy or compassion, we should breathe in and out in order to be aware of the joy and compassion in us. When we embrace our joy and our compassion with mindful breathing like this, they will be multiplied ten or twenty times. Mindful breathing helps us sustain them for a longer time and experience them more deeply. Therefore it is very important to embrace our positive mental formations, like joy, happiness, and compassion, when they arise, because they are a kind of food that helps us to grow. We speak of "the joy of meditation as daily food," because the feeling of joy arising from meditation, from mindfulness, nourishes and sustains us.

Similarly, when the mental formation that arises is negative, like anger or jealousy, we should go back to ourselves, and embrace it tenderly, calming it with our mindful breathing, like a mother would soothe her feverish child. So, "Breathing in, I calm my mental formations. Breathing out, I calm my mental formations."

Seeds of Anger, Seeds of Compassion

We often talk about consciousness as soil. The seeds of all mental formations are buried in our store consciousness. These mental formations are born, arise in our mind consciousness, remain for some time, and then return to the store consciousness in the form of a seed.

Our compassion also rests in our store consciousness in the form of a seed. Every time we touch or water a seed, it will spring up and manifest itself in our mind consciousness, the upper level of consciousness. If a positive seed, like the seed of joy or compassion, is watered and manifests, it will make us feel happy. But if a negative seed, like the seed of jealousy, is watered and manifests, it will make us feel unhappy. As long as our joy or anger is buried in the soil and no one touches it, we call it a seed. But when it manifests in mind consciousness, we call it a mental formation. We have to recognize anger in both its forms: as a seed in our store consciousness and as a mental formation, an active zone of energy that comes up in our mind consciousness. We have to realize that even when anger does not manifest, it is still there.

Everyone has a seed of anger in the depth of his or her consciousness. When that seed does not manifest, you don't feel angry at all. You don't feel angry with anyone. You feel fine, you feel fresh, you look lovely. You smile, laugh, and talk. But this does not mean that anger is not in you. Anger may not be manifesting in your mind consciousness, but it is always there in your store consciousness. If someone does something or says something that touches the seed of anger in you, it will manifest very quickly in the living room.

A good practitioner is not someone who no longer has any anger or suffering. This is not possible. A good practitioner is someone who knows how to take good care of her anger and suffering as soon as they arise. Someone who does not practice does not know how to handle the energy of anger when it manifests, and he or she can easily be overwhelmed by anger.

But if you practice mindful living, you do not allow anger to overwhelm you like that. You invite the seed of mindfulness up to take care of your anger. Mindful breathing and walking will help you to do this.

Habit Energy and Mindful Breathing

We all have habit energy in us. We are intelligent enough to know that if we do something or say something based on our habit energy, we will damage our relationships. And yet, even with this intelligence, we still do things out of anger, we still say things out of anger. Therefore, many of us have caused a lot of suffering in our relationships with other people. After the damage has been done, you are full of regret and you vow that you will never do such a thing again. You are very sincere; you have a great deal of good will. But the next time the situation presents itself, you do exactly the same thing, you say exactly the same thing, and you cause the same damage again and again.

Your intelligence, your knowledge, does not help you change your habit energy. Only the practice of recognizing, embracing, and transforming can help. That is why the Buddha advised us to practice mindful breathing to recognize and take care of our habit energy as soon as it manifests. If you are capable of embracing your habit energy with the energy of mindfulness, then you are safe, you are not going to make the same mistake again.

There was a young American friend who came to Plum Village and enjoyed the practice very much during his three weeks with us. He was very stable, compassionate, and understanding during his stay. One day, he was asked by the monks to go shopping for the community in preparation for Thanksgiving. While doing the shopping, he suddenly realized that he was rushing and wanted everything to be done very quickly so that he could go back to Plum Village.

This was the first time during the whole three weeks that he felt this kind of feeling: of rushing, of wanting everything to be done quickly. In Plum Village, he was surrounded by brothers practicing with solidity. He profited from their energy, and so the habit energy of rushing, of becoming stressed, never had a chance to manifest. Shopping in town, he was alone. He did not have the same kind of energy supporting him, so the seed of his habit energy arose right away.

Very quickly, he was able to recognize this habit energy

and realize that it had been transmitted to him by his mother. His mother was always rushing, wanting everything to be done quickly, quickly, quickly. With this insight, he returned to the practice of mindful breathing and said, "Hello Mom, I know you are there." After he had done this, the energy of rushing just vanished. He recognized his habit energy, embraced it mindfully, and was able to transform it. He regained the peace and solidity that he experienced before he left the community. He knew he was only able to do this because of his practice at Plum Village.

All of us are capable of doing this. Whenever our habit energy comes up, all we need to do is recognize it and call it by its name. We breathe mindfully and say, "Hello, my jealousy; hello, my fear; hello, my irritation and anger. I know you are there, and I am here for you. I will take good care of you and embrace you with mindfulness." Breathing in, we greet our habit energy, and breathing out we smile towards it. When we do this, our habit energy can no longer dominate us. We are safe. We have liberated ourselves.

ELEVEN

RESTORING THE PURE LAND

Making Happiness a Priority

From time to time we have to make a decision, and sometimes the decision is very difficult. We are forced to make a painful choice. But if we know what is most important to us, what we most deeply want for our life, the decision-making will become easier, and we won't have to suffer a lot.

When a person wants to become a monastic, for instance, it is not an easy decision. If your desire to be a monastic is less than one hundred percent, don't become a monastic. It must be more than one hundred percent. When you feel that monastic life is what you want more than anything else, other things become less important and the decision becomes much easier.

I have written three volumes on the history of Buddhism in Vietnam. All three volumes have been well received by readers. There is one more to write, the fourth volume. It's very important: the history of Buddhism in Vietnam from 1964 to the present. Writing this book is a very exciting and interesting project. I have lived through this period and so have gained firsthand experience. If I don't write it, there might not be anyone else with the time or the direct experience to do it. And this would do some injustice to history. Writing this book would also help people to learn more about the development and practice of Buddhism.

In me there is a historian. And I feel great joy when I play this role: making discoveries, revealing things that are new to other people, and giving the younger generation a direction to go in. They can learn a lot from the mistakes and the successes of past generations. So the desire to write this fourth volume is very strong. But I have not been able to write it because there are many more urgent things to do, such as helping relieve the suffering of people right beside me, in front of me, and around me. I cannot afford to be a scholar, a historian, although I know that this book is very important. I have all the documents needed for writing the book, but I would need one year to complete it. Which would mean no retreats, no dharma talks, no consultations, and so on.

We all have many things to do in our daily life. You have to decide which things are the most important to you. Getting a university degree may take you six or even eight years, and that is quite a long period of time. You may believe that this degree is important for your happiness. It might be, but perhaps there are other elements that are more important to your well-being, and to your happiness. You can work on improving the relationship between you and your father, your mother, or your partner. Do you have time for this? Can you afford enough time in order to do this work? It is very important to improve the relationship between you and your beloved ones. You are willing to put aside six years for a diploma; do you have the wisdom to use just as much time to work out a relationship? To deal with your anger? This time will bring you and the other person the happiness and stability you need to restore communication.

Writing a Book on Yourself

Recently, a university professor from the United States came to Plum Village. He was very eager to write a book on Thomas Merton and myself. He wanted to talk to me about it, and I said immediately, "Why don't you write a book on yourself? Why don't you invest one hundred percent of yourself into the practice of making yourself and the people around you happy? That is more important than writing a book on Thomas Merton and myself. Many books have been written on Thomas Merton already." Our friend said, with the best intentions and a lot of love, "But no one has written a book on you yet." I answered, "I don't care about a book on me, but I care very much about you writing a book on yourself. Write with your whole heart to transform yourself into an instrument of dharma, of the practice, so that you can become a free person, a happy person. That way you can help many people around you to be happy also."

What is most important to me is to establish a good relationship between my students and myself. I have to make it possible for people to practice and to transform. This is very rewarding and nourishing. Every time a practitioner is capable of transforming her suffering, and able to establish a good relationship with others, it is quite a victory. Not only a victory for him or for her, but a victory for the whole community, and for the practice as well. This is very nourishing for all of us. We know the story of the young nun in Plum Village who was able to help a mother and daughter reconcile. That was a real victory. It strengthened her faith in the practice and ours at the same time.

If you have difficulties with another person, and think that she only wants to make you suffer, and that it's impossible to do anything to help her, then you are not putting the teachings into practice. If it seems impossible for you to have a dialogue with her, that's because you lack experience in the practice. It is possible for you to talk to that person. Many people ask the question—"What if the other person doesn't want to cooperate, doesn't want to listen?" If the other person doesn't want to listen to you, to talk to you, or to work it out with you right now, then continue to practice and transform yourself so that reconciliation will be possible.

Writing a book on yourself is a way of looking deeply to recognize the roots of your suffering and find ways to transform them. It will help you become a free and happy person, able to make others around you happy also.

Nectar of Compassion

You should nourish yourself with the nectar of compassion before you approach another person in order to reconcile. Compassion is born from understanding—understanding that the other person also suffers. We tend to forget this. We see only our own suffering, and then we exaggerate, thinking, "No one else suffers like I do; I am the only one who suffers like this." But with a community to support you, you will be able to look deeper, to see that the other person also suffers very much.

It may be that because the other person has not had enough support, he has not been able to advance on the path of practice, and you have not helped him either. You are not even able to help yourself. But the teachings are exactly for that, the community is exactly for that—for nourishing ourselves with the nectar of compassion. We have to call on the dharma, we have to call on the sangha to help us. The dharma is effective in the here and the now.

Leaving the Prison of Notions

You should not practice like a machine, but with intelligence, so that each step, each breath, will make you feel better. Each mindful meal, each cup of tea, can make you feel better. Touch the wonders of life within and around you. Nourish yourself by allowing the beautiful and healing elements around you to penetrate you. This is the most important thing to do.

Ideas are not nourishing. In fact, ideas and notions very often become obstacles. They can become a prison. We must leave these ideas and notions behind in order to touch life, so full of wonders. Learn from your fellow practitioners who are capable of being happy, capable of loving. There are such people. They don't have problems with other members of their community because they can accept everyone. They are content. We have to cultivate the capacity of being happy like them. Living in the same environment, we share the same conditions of happiness. Others are capable of being happy, why can't we? What kind of obstacle is preventing us from being happy?

A Crucial Letter

If you have been trained in loving speech and deep listening, you can resolve a conflict with someone else by speaking to him or her directly. But if you are unsure whether your peace, solidity, and compassion are enough to keep you fresh, loving, and calm while you speak, then you may like to practice writing a letter. Writing a letter is a very important practice. Because even if you have the best of intentions, if your practice is not solid enough, you may become irritated when you speak and react in an unskillful way. This can ruin your chance. So sometimes it's safer and easier to write a letter.

In a letter you can be perfectly honest. You can tell the other person that there are things that she has done that have made you suffer, that have hurt you. You can write everything you feel inside. As you write, your practice is to be calm, to use the language of peace, of loving-kindness. Try to establish dialogue. You can write things like "My dear friend, I may be the victim of wrong perceptions, and what I write here may not reflect the truth. However, this is my experience of the situation. This is what I really feel in my heart. If there is anything wrong in what I write, let us sit down and look into it together so that we can clarify the misunderstanding."

In our tradition, when the monks and the nuns come together to offer guidance to someone who has requested it, they always use this kind of language. They use the insight of the community. This does not mean that the community's vision is perfect, but it is the best insight they can offer us. So the brothers and sisters acknowledge in their response that "As we offer this guidance, we are aware there may be things that we have not understood. There may be positive things in you that we have not seen. And there may be some wrong perception on the part of the community." So when you write a letter to the other person, do the same: "If my perceptions are not right, then please correct me." Use loving speech when you write. If one sentence is not written well enough, you can always begin anew and write another sentence that is more kind.

In the letter, we have to demonstrate that we have the capacity to see the suffering in the other person: "Dear friend, I know that you have suffered. And I know that you are not wholly responsible for your suffering." Because you have practiced looking deeply, you have discovered a number of different roots and causes of the other person's suffering. You can tell him all these things. You can tell him of your own suffering, and show that you understand why he acted or spoke the way he did.

Take one, two, or even three weeks to finish your letter, because it is a very important letter. It is more important than the fourth volume on the history of Buddhism in Vietnam. More important than the book on Thich Nhat Hanh and Thomas Merton. That letter is crucial for your happiness. The time you spend writing it is even more important than the one or two years you spend writing your doctoral thesis. Your thesis is not as crucial as this letter. Writing a letter like this is the best thing you can do to have a breakthrough and restore communication.

You are not alone in doing this. You have brothers and sisters who can shine light on you and help you with your letter. The people you need are right there with you in your community. When we write a book, we give the manuscript to friends, to specialists in order to ask for advice. Your fellow practitioners are specialists, because they all practice deep listening, deep looking, and loving speech.

You are the best doctor, you are the best therapist for your beloved one. So show the letter to a sister and ask her to tell you whether the language is kind enough, calm enough, and whether the insight is deep enough. After you show it to one brother or sister, you can still show it to another brother or sister until you feel that your letter will bring about a transformation in the other person and heal him.

How much of your time, energy, and love will you invest in such a letter? And who would refuse to help you in this important endeavor? It is crucial that you restore communication with this person whom you care so much about. It may be your father, your mother, your daughter, or your partner. He or she may be sitting right next to you.

Restoring the Pure Land

In the beginning of your relationship, the other person made a commitment to love and take care of you, but now, he's very, very distant. He doesn't want to look at you anymore. He doesn't want to hold your hand and walk with you anymore, and you suffer. In the beginning of your relationship, you felt you were in paradise. He fell in love with you, and you were so happy. Now it seems like he does not love you anymore and that he has abandoned you. He may be looking for another person, another relationship. Your paradise has become hell and you cannot get out of your hell.

Where does that hell come from? Is there someone pushing you into that hell and keeping you there? Perhaps hell is created by your mind, by your notions, by your wrong perceptions. So it is only with your mind that you can destroy the hell, and free yourself.

The practice of mindfulness, of recognizing and embracing anger is to open the door of your hell and transform it, rescuing yourself and the other person, returning together to the land of peace. This is possible and you are the one who is going to do it. Your friends who practice will, of course, support you with their insight, their energy of mindfulness and loving-kindness.

If you succeed in restoring the relationship, making the other person and yourself happy again, you make a great contribution. Everyone enjoys the victory, because everyone gains more faith in the practice. With support you can transform your hell and restore the Pure Land, restore peace in your daily life. You can start straightaway. You can begin to write that letter today. You will find out that with just a pencil and a sheet of paper, you can practice and transform your relationship.

Writing Your Letter All Day Long

While you're sitting, doing walking meditation, working, cleaning, or cooking a meal, don't think about the letter. But everything you do will be related to the letter.

The time you spend at your desk writing is only the time of putting your feelings on paper. But this is not exactly the moment that you produce the letter. You produce the letter when you water the vegetables, when you practice walking meditation, when you cook for the community. All these practices help you become more solid, more peaceful. The mindfulness and concentration you generate can help the seed of understanding and compassion in you to grow. When your letter comes from the mindfulness you have been generating all day long, then it will be a wonderful letter.

Live Each Moment Beautifully

About fifteen years ago, an American Buddhist scholar visited me while I was in the United States. She said, "Dear teacher, you write such beautiful poems. You spend a lot of time growing lettuce and doing things like that. Why don't you use your time to write more poetry?" She had read somewhere that I enjoy growing vegetables, taking care of cucumber and lettuce. She was thinking pragmatically and suggested that I should not waste my time working in the garden but should use it to write poems.

I replied, "My dear friend, if I did not grow lettuce, I could not write the poems I write." This is the truth. If you don't live in concentration, in mindfulness, if you don't live every moment of your daily life deeply, then you cannot write. You can't produce anything valuable to offer to others.

A poem is a flower you offer to people. A compassionate look, a smile, an act filled with loving-kindness is also a flower that blooms on the tree of mindfulness and concentration. Even though you don't think about the poem while cooking lunch for your family, the poem is being written. When I write a short story, a novel, or a play, it may take one week or several weeks to finish. But the story or the novel is always there. In the same way, although you are not thinking about the letter you will write to your beloved one, the letter is being written, deep down in your consciousness.

You cannot just sit there and write the story or the novel. You have to do other things as well. You drink tea, cook breakfast, wash your clothes, water the vegetables. The time spent doing these things is extremely important. You have to do them well. You have to put one hundred percent of yourself into the act of cooking, watering the vegetable garden, of dish washing. You just enjoy whatever you are doing, and you do it deeply. This is very important for your story, your letter, or anything else that you want to produce.

Enlightenment is not separate from washing dishes or growing lettuce. To learn how to live each moment of our daily life in deep mindfulness and concentration is the practice. The conception and unfolding of a piece of art take place exactly in these moments of our daily life. The time when you begin to write down the music or the poems is only the time of delivering the baby. The baby has to be in you already in order for you to deliver it. But if the baby is not in you, even if you sit for hours and hours at your desk, there's nothing to deliver, and you cannot produce anything. Your insight, your compassion, and your ability to write in a way that will move the other person's heart are flowers that bloom on your tree of practice. We should make good use of every moment of our daily life in order to allow this insight and compassion to bloom.

The Gift of Transformation

A pregnant mother can be very happy every time she thinks of the baby inside of her. The baby, although not born yet, can give the mother a lot of joy. Every moment of her daily life, she is aware of the baby's presence, so she does everything with love. She eats with love, she drinks with love because she knows that without her love, the baby may not be healthy. She's very careful all the time. She knows that if she makes a mistake, if she smokes a lot, if she drinks a lot of alcohol, this will not be good for her baby. So she's very mindful, and she lives with the mind of love.

Practitioners have to act very much like a mother. We know that we want to produce something, we want to offer something to humanity, to the world. Each of us carries within ourselves a baby—the baby Buddha, and it is the baby Buddha in us that we can offer. We must live in mindfulness in order to take good care of our baby Buddha.

It is the energy of the Buddha in us that allows us to write a real love letter and reconcile with another person. A real love letter is made of insight, understanding, and compassion. Otherwise it is not a love letter. A true love letter can produce a transformation in the other person, and therefore in the world. But before it produces a transformation in the other person, it has to produce a transformation within you. The time you take to write the letter may be your whole life.

APPENDIX A

At Plum Village, couples, family members, or friends often sign this treaty in a ceremony in which the whole community is present. However, you can adapt it in any way that makes you feel comfortable. At the end are Buddhist references, but please feel free to change them to match your own spiritual tradition.

PEACE TREATY

In Order That We May Live Long and Happily Together, In Order That We May Continually Develop and Deepen Our Love and Understanding, We, the Undersigned, Vow to Observe and Practice the Following:

I, the one who is angry, agree to:

1. Refrain from saying or doing anything that might cause further damage or escalate the anger.
2. Not suppress my anger.

3. Practice mindful breathing and go back to myself to take care of my anger.

4. Calmly, within twenty-four hours, tell the one who has made me angry about my anger and suffering, either verbally or by delivering a Peace Note.

5. Ask for an appointment later in the week, like Friday evening, either verbally or by note, to discuss this matter more thoroughly.

6. Not say: "I am not angry, it's okay, I am not suffering. There is nothing to be angry about."

7. Look deeply into my daily life, while sitting, walking, lying down, working, and driving in order to see:

The ways that I myself, have been unskillful at times.

How I have hurt the other person because of my own habit energy.

How the strong seed of anger in me is the primary cause of my anger.

How the other person is only the secondary cause.

How the other person is only seeking relief from his or her suffering.

That as long as the other person suffers, I cannot be truly happy.

8. Apologize immediately, without waiting for the Friday appointment, as soon as I recognize my unskillfulness and lack of mindfulness.

9. Postpone the Friday meeting if I do not feel calm enough to meet with the other person.

I, the one who has made the other angry, agree to:

1. Respect the other person's feelings, not ridicule him/her and allow enough time for him/her to calm down.

2. Not press for an immediate discussion.

3. Confirm the other person's request for a meeting, either verbally or by note, and assure him or her that I will be there.

4. If I can apologize, do so right away and not wait until Friday evening.

5. Practice mindful breathing and deep looking to see how:

I have seeds of anger and unkindness as well as the habit energy, which make the other person unhappy. I have mistakenly thought that making the other person suffer would relieve my own suffering. By making him/her suffer, I make myself suffer.

6. Apologize as soon as I realize my unskillfulness and lack of mindfulness, without making any attempt to justify myself and without waiting for the Friday meeting.

We Vow with the Presence of the Lord Buddha as Witness
and the Mindful Presence of Our Sangha,
to Abide by
These Articles and Practice Them Wholeheartedly. We
Invoke the Three Gems for Protection to Grant
us Clarity and Confidence.

Signed, _____

_____

The ____ Day of _____ in the Year _____ at _____.

—◦◦∞◦◦—

THE FIVE MINDFULNESS TRAININGS

The First Mindfulness Training: Reverence for Life

Aware of the suffering caused by the destruction of life, I vow to cultivate compassion and learn ways to protect the lives of people, animals, plants, and minerals. I am determined not to kill, not to let others kill, and not to condone any act of killing in the world, in my thinking, or in my way of life.

The Second Mindfulness Training: Generosity

Aware of the suffering caused by exploitation, social injustice, stealing, and oppression, I vow to cultivate loving-kindness and learn ways to work for the well-being of people, animals, plants, and minerals. I vow to practice generosity by sharing my time, energy, and material resources with those who are in real need. I am determined not to steal and not to possess anything that should belong to others. I will respect the property of others, but I will prevent others from profiting from human suffering or the suffering of other species on earth.

The Third Mindfulness Training:
Sexual Responsibility

Aware of the suffering caused by sexual misconduct, I vow to cultivate responsibility and learn ways to protect the safety and integrity of individuals, couples, families, and society. I am determined not to engage in sexual relations without love and a long-term commitment. To preserve the happiness of myself and others, I am determined to respect my commitments and the commitments of others. I will do everything in my power to protect children from sexual abuse and to protect couples and families from being broken by sexual misconduct.

The Fourth Mindfulness Training: Deep Listening and Loving Speech

Aware of the suffering caused by unmindful speech and the inability to listen to others, I vow to cultivate loving speech and deep listening in order to bring joy and happiness to others and relieve others of their suffering. Knowing that words can create happiness or suffering, I vow to learn to speak truthfully with words that inspire self-confidence, joy, and hope. I am determined not to spread news that I do not know to be certain and not to criticize or condemn things of which I am not sure. I will refrain from uttering words that can cause division or discord, or that can cause the family or the community to break. I will make all efforts to reconcile and resolve all conflicts, however small.

The Fifth Mindfulness Training: Mindful Consumption

Aware of the suffering caused by unmindful consumption, I vow to cultivate good health, both physical and mental, for myself, my family, and my society by practicing mindful eating, drinking, and consuming. I vow to ingest only items that preserve peace, well-being, and joy in my body, in my consciousness, and in the collective body and consciousness of my family and society. I am determined not to use alcohol or any other intoxicant or to ingest food or other items that contain toxins, such as certain TV programs, magazines, books, films, and conversations. I am aware that to damage my body or my consciousness with these poisons is to betray my ancestors, my parents, my society, and future generations. I will work to transform violence, fear, anger, and confusion in myself and in society by practicing a diet for myself and for society. I understand that a proper diet is crucial for self-transformation and for the transformation of society.

GUIDED MEDITATIONS FOR LOOKING DEEPLY AND RELEASING ANGER

You may find these guided meditations helpful in practicing the teachings you have received on transforming anger. You can guide yourself through them silently or invite someone else to guide the meditations, reading the exercises out loud.

Begin with "Breathing in, I know I am breathing in. Breathing out, I know I am breathing out." Followed by the key words "In, out." You should always start with a few moments of mindful breathing to calm your mind. Use the first key word to accompany the in-breath, and the second key word to accompany the out-breath. Repeat these key words silently with your in- and out-breath in order to really touch the meaning of the meditation. Avoid saying the words mechanically; instead experience and feel them concretely. Allow eight to ten in- and out-breaths for each exercise, keeping the key words alive during each in- and out-breath.

Looking Deeply at Anger

1. Contemplating a person in anger, I breathe in.   Angry person
   Seeing the suffering of that person, I breathe out.   Suffering

2. Contemplating the damage from anger to self and others, I breathe in.   Anger harms self and others
   Seeing that anger burns and destroys happiness, I breathe out.

   Destroys happiness

3. Seeing anger's roots in my body, I breathe in.   Anger's roots in body
   Seeing anger's roots in my consciousness, I breathe out.   Anger's roots in consciousness

4. Seeing the roots of anger in
wrong perceptions and
ignorance, breathe in.
Smiling to my wrong
perceptions and ignorance, I
breathe out.

Anger's roots in
wrong perceptions
and ignorance

Smiling

5. Seeing the angry person
suffer, I breathe in.
Feeling compassion for the
angry person who suffers,
I breathe out.

Angry person suffers

Feeling compassion

6. Seeing the unfavorable
environment and
unhappiness of the angry
person, I breathe in.
Understanding the causes of
this unhappiness, I breathe
out.

Angry person
unhappy

Understanding
unhappiness

7. Seeing myself burned by the
fire of anger, I breathe in.

Burned by anger

Feeling compassion for
myself burning with anger,
I breathe out.

Compassion for
myself

8. Knowing anger makes me
look ugly, I breathe in.
Seeing myself as the chief
cause of my ugliness, I
breathe out.

Anger makes me
ugly

I cause my ugliness

9. Seeing when I am angry I am
a burning house, I breathe in.
Taking care of my anger and
going back to myself,
I breathe out.

I am a burning
house

Taking care of
myself

10. Contemplating helping the
angry person, I breathe in.
Seeing myself able to help
the angry person, I breathe
out.

Helping angry
person

Capable of helping

Releasing Anger and Healing Relations with Our Parents

I. Seeing myself as a five-year-
old child, I breathe in.
Smiling to the five-year-old
child, I breathe out.

Myself, five years old

Smiling

2. Seeing the five-year-old child
as fragile and vulnerable, I
breathe in.
Smiling with love to the five-
year-old in me, I breathe out.

Five-year-old, fragile

Smiling with love

3. Seeing my father as a five-
year-old boy, I breathe in.
Smiling to my father as a
five-year-old boy, I breathe
out.

Father, five years old

Smiling

4. Seeing my five-year-old
father as fragile and
vulnerable, I breathe in.
Smiling with love and

Father, fragile and
vulnerable

understanding to my father
as a five-year-old boy, I
breathe out.

Smiling with love
and understanding

5. Seeing my mother as a five-
year-old girl, I breathe in.
Smiling to my mother as a
five-year-old girl, I breathe
out.

Mother, five years
old

Smiling

6. Seeing my five-year-old
mother as fragile and
vulnerable, I breathe in.
Smiling with love and
understanding to my mother
as a five-year-old girl, I
breathe out.

Mother, fragile and
vulnerable

Smiling with love
and understanding

7. Seeing my father suffering as
a child, I breathe in.
Seeing my mother suffering
as a child, I breathe out.

Father, suffering as
a child
Mother, suffering as
a child

8. Seeing my father in me, I
   breathe in.   Father in me
   Smiling to my father in me,
   I breathe out.   Smiling

9. Seeing my mother in me, I
   breathe in.   Mother in me
   Smiling to my mother in me,
   I breathe out.   Smiling

10. Understanding the
    difficulties that my father in
    me has, I breathe in.   Difficulties of father
    Determined to work for the   in me
    release of both my father
    and me, I breathe out.   Releasing father
                                        and me

11. Understanding the
    difficulties that my mother
    in me has, I breathe in.   Difficulties of
    Determined to work for the   mother in me
    release of both my mother
    and me, I breathe out.   Releasing mother
                                        and me

APPENDIX D

——◦∞◦——

DEEP RELAXATION

This is an example of how to guide yourself or others in Deep Relaxation. Allowing your body to rest is very important. When your body is at ease and relaxed, your mind will also be at peace. The practice of Deep Relaxation is essential for your body and mind to heal. Please take the time to practice it often. Although the following guided relaxation may take you thirty minutes, feel free to modify it to fit your situation. You can make it shorter—just five or ten minutes when you wake up in the morning, before going to bed in the evening, or during a short break in the middle of a busy day. You can also make it longer and more in-depth. The most important thing is to enjoy it.

Lie down comfortably on your back on the floor or on a bed.

Close your eyes. Allow your arms to rest gently on either side of your body and let your legs relax, turning outwards.

As you breathe in and out, become aware of your whole body lying down. Feel all the areas of your body that are touching the floor or the bed you are lying on; your heels, the backs of your legs, your buttocks, your back, the back of your hands and arms, the back of your head. With each out-breath, feel yourself sink deeper and deeper into the floor, letting go of tension, letting go of worries, not holding on to anything.

As you breathe in, feel your abdomen rising, and as your breathe out, feel your abdomen falling. For several breaths, just notice the rise and fall of your abdomen.

Now, as you breathe in, become aware of your two feet. As you breathe out, allow your two feet to relax. Breathing in, send your love to your feet, and breathing out, smile to your feet. As you breathe in and out, know how wonderful it is to have two feet, that allow you to walk, to run, to play sports, to dance, to drive, to do so many activities throughout the day. Send your gratitude to your two feet for always being there for you whenever you need them.

Breathing in, become aware of your right and left legs. Breathing out, allow all the cells in your legs to relax. Breathing in, smile to your legs, and breathing out, send them your love. Appreciate whatever degree of strength and health is there in your legs. As you breathe in and out, send them your tenderness and care. Allow them to rest, sinking gently into the floor. Release any tension you may be holding in your legs.

Breathing in, become aware of your two hands lying on the floor. Breathing out, completely relax all the muscles in your two hands, releasing any tension you may be holding in them. As you breathe in, appreciate how wonderful it is to have two hands. As you breathe out, send a smile of love to your two hands. Breathing in and out, be in touch with all the things your two hands allow you to do: to cook, to write, to drive, to hold the hand of someone else, to hold a baby, to wash your own body, to draw, to play a musical instrument, to type, to build and fix things, to pet an animal, to hold a cup of tea. So many things are available to you because of your two hands. Just enjoy the fact that you have two hands and allow all the cells in your hands to really rest.

Breathing in, become aware of your two arms. Breathing out, allow your arms, to fully relax. As you breathe in, send your love to your arms, and as you breathe out, smile to them. Take the time to appreciate your arms and whatever strength and health are there in your arms. Send them your gratitude for allowing you to hug someone else, to swing on a swing, to help and serve others, to work hard—cleaning the house, mowing the lawn, to do so many things throughout the day.

Breathing in and out, allow your two arms to let go and rest completely on the floor. With each out-breath, feel the tension leaving your arms. As you embrace your arms with your mindfulness, feel joy and ease in every part of your two arms.

Breathing in, become aware of your shoulders. Breathing out, allow any tension in your shoulders to flow out into the floor. As you breathe in, send your love to your shoulders, and as you breathe out, smile with gratitude to them. Breathing in and out, be aware that you may have allowed a lot of tension and stress to accumulate in your shoulders. With each exhalation, allow the tension to leave your shoulders, feeling them relax more and more deeply. Send them your tenderness and care, knowing that you do not want to put too much strain on them, but that you want to live in a way that will allow them to be relaxed and at ease.

Breathing in, become aware of your heart. Breathing out, allow your heart to rest. With your in-breath, send your love to your heart. With your out-breath, smile to your heart. As you breathe in and out, get in touch with how wonderful it is to have a heart still beating in your chest. Your heart allows your life to be possible, and it is always there for you, every minute, every day. It never takes a break. Your heart has been beating since you were a four-week-old fetus in your mother's womb. It is a marvelous organ that allows you to do everything you do throughout the day. Breathe in and know that your heart also loves you. Breathe out and commit to live in a way that will help your heart to function well. With each exhalation, feel your heart relaxing more and more. Allow each cell in your heart to smile with ease and joy.

Breathing in, become aware of your stomach and intestines. Breathing out, allow your stomach and intestines to relax. As you breathe in, send them your love and gratitude. As you breathe out, smile tenderly to them. Breathing in and out, know how essential these organs are to your health. Give them the chance to rest deeply. Each day they digest and assimilate the food you eat, giving you energy and strength. They need you to take the time to recognize and appreciate them. As you breathe in, feel your stomach and intestines relaxing and releasing all tension. As you breathe out, enjoy the fact that you have a stomach and intestines.

Breathing in, become aware of your eyes. Breathing out, allow your eyes and the muscles around your eyes to relax. Breathing in, smile to your eyes, and breathing out, send them your love. Allow your eyes to rest and roll back into your head. As you breathe in and out, know how precious your two eyes are. They allow you to look into the eyes of someone you love, to see a beautiful sunset, to read and write, to move around with ease, to see a bird flying in the sky, to watch a movie—so many things are possible because of your two eyes. Take the time to appreciate the gift of sight and allow your eyes to rest deeply. You can gently raise your eyebrows to help release any tension you may be holding around your eyes.

Here you can continue to relax other areas of your body, using the same pattern as above.

Now, if there is a place in your body that is sick or in pain, take this time to become aware of it and send it your love. Breathing in, allow this area to rest, and breathing out, smile to it with great tenderness and affection. Be aware that there are other parts of your body that are still strong and healthy. Allow these strong parts of your body to send their strength and energy to the weak or sick area. Feel the support, energy, and love of the rest of your body penetrating the weak area, soothing and healing it. Breathe in and affirm your own capacity to heal, breathe out and let go of the worry or fear you may be holding in your body. Breathing in and out, smile with love and confidence to the area of your body that is not well.

Finally, breathing in, become aware of the whole of your body lying down. Breathing out, enjoy the sensation of your whole body lying down, very relaxed and calm. Smile to your whole body as you breathe in, and send your love and compassion to your whole body as you breathe out. Feel all the cells in your whole body smiling joyfully with you. Feel gratitude for all the cells in your whole body. Return the gentle rise and fall of your abdomen.

If you are guiding other people, and if you are comfortable doing so, you can now sing a few relaxing songs or lullabies.

To end, slowly stretch and open your eyes. Take your time to get up, calmly and lightly. Practice to carry the calm and mindful energy you have generated into your next activity and throughout the day.

Thich Nhat Hanh has lived an extraordinary life in an extra-ordinary time. Since the age of sixteen he has been a Buddhist monk, a peace activist, and a seeker of the way. He has survived persecution, three wars, and more than thirty years of exile. He is the master of a temple in Vietnam whose lineage goes back over two thousand years and, indeed, is traceable to Buddha himself. The author of more than one hundred books of poetry, fiction, and philosophy, Thich Nhat Hanh has founded universities and social service organizations, and rescued boat people; he led the Vietnamese Buddhist delegation at the Paris Peace Talks and was nominated for the Nobel Peace Prize by the Reverend Martin Luther King, Jr. He makes his home in France and Vermont.

Thich Nhat Hanh has retreat communities in southwestern France (Plum Village), Vermont (Green Mountain Dharma Center), and California (Deer Park), where monks, nuns, laymen, and laywomen practice the art of mindful living. Visitors are invited to join the practice for at least one week. For information, please write to:

Plum Village
13 Martineau
33580 Dieulivol
France
NH-office@plumvillage.org *(for women)*
LH-office@plumvillage.org *(for women)*
UH-office@plumvillage.org *(for men)*
www.plumvillage.org

For information about our monasteries, mindfulness practice centers, and retreats in the United States please contact:

Green Mountain Dharma Center
P.O. Box 182
Hartland Four Corners, VT 05049
Tel: (802) 436–1103
Fax: (802) 436–1101
MF-office@plumvillage.org
www.plumvillage.org

Deer Park Monastery
2499 Melru Lane
Escondido, CA 92026
Tel: (760) 291–1003
Fax: (760) 291–1172
Deerpark@plumvillage.org

Also available from Rider . . .

THE MIRACLE OF MINDFULNESS
A Manual on Meditation
Thich Nhat Hanh

This lucid and beautifully written guide to Eastern meditation explains how to acquire the skills of mindfulness — of being awake and fully aware. Modern medical research has shown the positive effects of meditation for psychological and spiritual health, and the reader will need no particular religious orientation to benefit from the wisdom of this manual. Thich Nhat Hanh's gentle anecdotes and practical exercises will help both beginners and advanced students arrive at greater self-understanding and peacefulness.

If you would like to order any of the following or to receive our catalogue please fill in the form below:

Also by Thich Nhat Hanh and available from Rider:

Fragrant Palm Leaves	£7.99
Going Home	£10.99
The Heart of the Buddha's Teaching	£10.99
Peace Is Every Step	£8.99
The Miracle of Mindfulness	£9.99
The Sun My Heart	£7.99
Transformation and Healing	£7.99
Present Moment, Wonderful Moment	£6.99
Living Buddha, Living Christ	£10.99
Being Peace	£6.99
Breathe! You Are Alive	£6.99
Old Path, White Clouds	£19.99

ALL RIDER BOOKS ARE AVAILABLE THROUGH MAIL ORDER OR FROM YOUR LOCAL BOOKSHOP.

PAYMENT MAY BE MADE USING ACCESS, VISA, MASTER-CARD, DINERS CLUB, SWITCH AND AMEX, OR CHEQUE, EUROCHEQUE AND POSTAL ORDER (STERLING ONLY).

EXPIRY DATE .... SWITCH ISSUE NO.

SIGNATURE ....

PLEASE ALLOW £2.50 FOR POST AND PACKING FOR THE FIRST BOOK AND £1.00 PER BOOK THEREAFTER.

ORDER TOTAL: £.. (INCLUDING P&P)

ALL ORDERS TO:
RIDER BOOKS, BOOKS BY POST, TBS LIMITED, THE BOOK SERVICE, COLCHESTER ROAD, FRATING GREEN, COLCHESTER, ESSEX, CO7 7DW, UK.

TELEPHONE: (01206) 256 000
FAX: (01206) 255 914

NAME ....

ADDRESS ....

....

Please allow 28 days for delivery. Please tick box if you do not wish to receive any additional information. □
Prices and availability subject to change without notice.